GW00494193

AAT

Qualifications and Credit Framework (QCF)

LEVEL 4 DIPLOMA IN ACCOUNTING

(QCF)

QUESTION BANK

Option Paper:
Business Tax
FA 2011

For assessments from 1 March 2012

First edition 2010

Second edition April 2011
Third edition September 2011

ISBN 9781 4453 7878 7

(Previous ISBN 9780 7517 9770 1)

British Library Cataloguing-in-Publication Data
A catalogue record for this book is available from the British
Library

Published by

BPP Learning Media Ltd
BPP House
Aldine Place
London W12 8AA

www.bpp.com/learningmedia

Printed in the United Kingdom

Your learning materials, published by BPP Learning Media Ltd,
are printed on paper sourced from sustainable, managed forests.

We are grateful to the AAT for permission to reproduce the
sample assessment. The answers to the sample assessment for
business tax have been published by the AAT. All other answers
have been prepared by BPP Learning Media Ltd.

CONTENTS

BPP note: Assessments under FA 2010 and F(No.2)A 2010 will cease to be available from 31 May 2012. This Question Bank covers the provisions from FA 2011. Assessments under FA 2011 will be available from 1 March 2012 through to 31 March 2013. Check the date you intend to sit the assessment to ensure you are using the correct material.

A NOTE ABOUT COPYRIGHT

INTRODUCTION

This is BPP Learning Media's AAT Question Bank for Business Tax. It is part of a suite of groundbreaking resources produced by BPP Learning Media for the AAT's assessments under the qualification and credit framework.

The business tax assessment is **computer assessed**. As well as being available in the traditional paper format, this **question bank is** provided to you *FREE OF CHARGE* **in an online form** where all questions and assessments are presented in a **style which mimics the style of the AAT's assessments.** BPP Learning Media believe that the best way to practise for an online assessment is in an online environment. However, if you are unable to practise in the online environment you will find that all tasks in the paper question bank have been written in a style that is as close as possible to the style that you will be presented with in your online assessment.

FOR FREE ACCESS TO THE ONLINE QUESTION BANK SCRATCH OFF THE SILVER STICKER AT THE FRONT OF THIS BOOK.

This Question Bank has been written in conjunction with the BPP Text, and has been carefully designed to enable students to practise all of the learning outcomes and assessment criteria for the unit that makes up Business Tax. It is fully up to date for Finance Act 2011 and reflects both the AAT's unit guide and the sample assessment provided by the AAT.

This Question Bank contains these key features:

- graded practice tasks corresponding to each of the main topics in Business Tax. Some tasks are designed for learning purposes, others are of assessment standard. Further details of the specific topics tested in each task are given on the next page.

- the AAT's sample assessment and answers for Business Tax and five further practice assessments

The emphasis in all tasks and assessments is on the practical application of the skills acquired.

If you have any comments about this book, please e-mail suedexter@bpp.com or write to Sue Dexter, Publishing Director, BPP Learning Media Ltd, BPP House, Aldine Place, London W12 8AA.

SPECIFIC TOPIC LIST

The practice tasks are grouped according to the main topics assessed in Business Tax. This table gives you a list of tasks dealing with specific topics to enable you to focus your task practice.

Topic	Practice tasks
Revenue or capital expenditure	1.1
Capital allowances for sole trader	1.2, 1.3. 1.4
Badges of trade	1.5
Adjustment of profit for sole trader	1.6, 1.7
Basis of assessment for sole trader	1.8, 1.9, 1.10, 1.11
Losses for sole trader	1.12, 1.13, 1.14, 1.15
National insurance contributions	1.16, 1.17, 1.18, 1.19, 2.5
Self employment tax return	1.20
Partnership allocation of profit	2.1, 2.2, 2.3, 2.4
Basis of assessment for partners	2.2, 2.5
Partnership tax return	2.6
Adjustment of profit for company	3.1, 3.2
Long period of account	3.3, 3.4
Capital allowances for company	3.5
Corporation tax calculation	3.6, 3.7, 3.8, 3.9
Losses for company	3.10, 3.11, 3.12, 3.13, 3.14
Corporation tax return	3.15
Chargeable gains definitions	4.1, 4.2, 5.8
Calculation of gains for individuals	4.3, 4.4
Capital losses	4.5, 4.9, 4.10
Capital gains tax payable	4.5, 4.6, 4.7, 4.8
Chattels	4.11, 4.12, 4.13, 5.4
Connected persons	4.14, 4.15
Share disposals by individuals	4.16, 4.17, 4.18
Entrepreneurs' relief	4.19, 4.20

Topic	Practice tasks
Gift relief	4.21, 4.22
Rollover relief	4.23, 5.7, 5.10
Calculation of gains for companies	5.1, 5.2, 5.3
Share disposals by companies	5.5, 5.6, 5.9
Filing date for return	6.1
Penalties and interest	6.3, 6.4, 6.5, 6.6, 6.7, 6.8, 6.9
Payment of tax by individuals	6.2, 6.9
Payment of tax by companies	6.8, 6.9

Question bank

Business Tax – Practice tasks

Sole traders

Task 1.1

For the following items of expenditure, tick if they are revenue or capital:

	Revenue	Capital
Purchase of machinery		✓
Rent paid for premises	✓	
Insurance of premises	✓	
Repairs to roof of factory	✓	
New extension to shop		✓
Purchase of new car for owner		✓
Legal fees relating to purchase of new factory		✓
Payment of staff wages	✓	
Accountancy costs	✓	
Redecoration of shop	✓	

....

Task 1.2

Bodie, a sole trader, makes up his accounts to 5 April each year. The value of the main pool as at 6 April 2011 was £38,500.

His expenditure, all qualifying for capital allowances, has been as follows:

Date		£	
14 July 2011	Office furniture	23,800 ✓ AIA
30 March 2012	Mercedes car – CO$_2$ emissions 150g/km Bus. 80%	18,000 OWN POOL
31 March 2012	Car – CO$_2$ emissions 130g/km	8,000 MAIN POOL
2 April 2012	Machinery	31,000 ✓ AIA

The Mercedes was for the proprietor's own use (20% private), while the other car was for an employee.

Machinery which had been acquired for £7,000 was sold for £3,000 on 29 March 2012.

Using the pro forma layout provided, calculate capital allowances for the year ending 5 April 2012.

Y/E 5 APRIL 2012	AIA	MAIN POOL	MERCEDES CAR 80%	ALLOWANCES
B/F		38,500		
AIA ADDITIONS				
14.7.11 FURNITURE	23,800			
2.4.12 MACHINERY	31,000			
	54,800			
AIA	(54,800)			54,800
NON AIA ADDITIONS				
30.3.12 CAR			18,000	
30.3.12 CAR		8000		
DISPOSALS				
29.3.12 MACHINERY		(3000)		
		43,500		
WDA @ 20%		(8700)		8,700
WDA @ 20%			(3600)	2,880
C/F		34,800	14,400	
ALLOWANCES				66,380

Task 1.3

Wolfgang commences to trade on 6 January 2011. During his first year, he incurs the following expenditure:

		£
6 January 2011	Machinery	112,000
6 July 2011	Car with CO_2 emissions of 105g/km	8,000
31 October 2011	Car with CO_2 emissions of 155g/km	10,500

Using the pro forma layout provided, compute the capital allowance available to Wolfgang for the year ended 5 January 2012.

Y/E 5 JAN 2012	AIA	FYA 100%	MAIN POOL	ALLOWANCES
AIA ADDITIONS				
6.1.11 MACHINERY	112,000			
AIA	(100,000)			100,000
	12,000			
TRANSFER TO MAIN POOL	(12,000)		12,000	
FYA @ 100%				
6.7.11 LOW EMISSION CAR		8000		
FYA @ 100%		(8000)		8000
		—		
NON AIA ADDITION				
31.10.11 CAR			10,500	
			22,500	
WDA @ 20%			(4500)	4500
c/f			18,000	
ALLOWANCES				112,500

Task 1.4

Rachel is a sole trader making up accounts to 30 April each year.

On 1 May 2010, the brought forward balances on her plant and machinery were as follows:

	£
Main pool	120,000
Car – private use 30% by Rachel	21,000
Car – no private use (acquired before 5 April 2009)	17,500

She sold the car used by her privately for £16,000 on 10 August 2010 and bought another car (CO_2 emissions 170g/km) on the same day for £25,000, which also had 30% private use by her.

Using the pro forma layout provided, calculate the capital allowances available in the year to 30 April 2011.

Y/E 30 APRIL 2011	MAIN POOL	70% CAR-1	CAR-2	70% CAR-3	ALLOWANCE
B/F	120,000	21,000	17,500		
NON AIA ADDITION					
10·8·10 CAR				25000	
DISPOSAL					
10 8 10 CAR		(16,000)			
BALANCING ALLOWANCE		5000			3500
WDA @ 20%	(24,000)				24000
WDA @ 20%			(3000)		3000
WDA @ 10%				(2500)	1750
C/F	96,000		14,500	22,500	~~32750~~
ALLOWANCES					32,250

Task 1.5

When deciding whether or not a trade is being carried on, HM Revenue and Customs is often guided by the badges of trade.

Write a memo to your manager explaining what you understand by the term badges of trade.

From:	AAT student
To:	Manager
Date:	14 June 2012
Subject:	Badges of trade

This page is for the continuation of your memo. You may not need all of it.

Task 1.6

The income statement (profit and loss account) of Mr Jelly for the year ended 31 December 2011 shows:

	£		£
Staff wages	2,500	Gross profit from trading account	10,000
Light and heat	300		
Motor car expenses	350		
Postage, stationery and telephone	100		
Repairs and renewals	450		
Impairment losses (bad debts)	100		
Miscellaneous expenses	300		
Depreciation	600✗		
Net profit	5,300		
	10,000		10,000

The following information is also relevant:

(1) The staff wages include £260 paid to Mr Jelly.✗
(2) One-seventh of the motor expenses relates to private motoring. ✗
(3) Repairs and renewals comprise:

	£
Painting shop internally ✓	129 ✓
Plant repairs ✓	220 ✓
Building extension to stockroom ✗	101 ✗
	450

(4) Impairment (bad debt) provisions

2011		£	2011		£
Dec 31	Impairment loss written-off	102	Jan 1	Balances b/f	
	Balances c/f			General	200
	General	400		Specific	360
	Specific	398			
			Dec 31	Impairment loss recovered	240
	200 INCREASE			Income statement	100
		900			900

9

(5) Miscellaneous expenses include:

	£
Donations – Oxfam	10 ✗
Advertising	115
Customer entertaining	90 ✗
Christmas gifts – ten bottles of gin and whisky	70 ✗
Legal expenses re debt collecting	15
	300

Using the pro forma layout provided, compute Mr Jelly's taxable trading profit for the year ended 31 December 2011.

PROFITS PER ACCOUNTS		5300
SALARY TO MR JELLY	260	
PRIVATE MOTORING	50	
STOCKROOM EXTENSION	101	
IMPAIRMENT PROVISION	200	
DONATION – OXFAM	10	
CUSTOMER ENTERTAINING	90	
CHRISTMAS GIFTS	70	
DEPRECIATION	600	
		1381
TAXABLE TRADING PROFIT		6681

Task 1.7

Brutus has been trading for many years as a retailer of the busts of Roman emperors.

His income statement (profit and loss account) for the year ended 31 December 2011 was as follows:

	£	£
Gross profit		50,000
Wages and salaries	18,000	
Repairs	4,550	
Depreciation	4,000 ✗	
Bank interest	300	
Impairment losses	700	
Legal expenses	400 ✗	
Rent and rates	2,450	
Entertaining	600	
		(31,000)
Net profit		19,000

The following items are relevant:

(1) Brutus took two busts of the emperor Trajan to give to friends which were valued as follows:

	£
Cost (each)	20
Market value (each)	2× 25 = 50 ✗

No entry has been made in the accounts in respect of the removal of the busts. (The original cost was correctly put through the accounts when the busts were purchased.)

(2) The Provision for Impairment Losses Account has been reconstructed as follows:

The provisions b/f and c/f can be analysed as follows:

		£
b/f	General	500
	Specific	800
c/f	General	470
	Specific	1,000

(30) DEDUCT ✗

All the debts were trade debts.

(3) Legal expenses were in connection with the proposed purchase of new freehold premises. It was eventually decided not to proceed with the purchase. ✗

(4) Entertaining has been analysed as follows:

	£
Staff party	325
Cocktail party held for customers	275 ✗
	600

Using the pro forma layout provided, compute Brutus' taxable trading profit for the year ended 31 December 2011.

PROFIT PER ACCOUNTS		19,000
GOODS TAKEN FOR OWN USE	50	
DEPRECIATION	4000	
LEGAL EXPENSES	400	
CUSTOMER ENTERTAINING	275	
		4725
DECREASE IN IMPAIRMENT LOSS PROVISION		(30)
TAXABLE TRADING PROFIT		23695

Task 1.8

Rachel commenced in business as a fashion designer on 1 January 2010, and made up her first accounts to 30 April 2011. Her profit for the period, adjusted for taxation, was £33,000. *16 MONTHS*

(1) Using the pro forma layout provided, calculate the taxable profit for the first three tax years.

Tax year	Basis period	Taxable profits
		£
2009/10	1/1/10 — 5/4/10 3/16	6188.00
2010/11	6/4/10 — 5/4/11	24750.00
2011/12	1/5/10 — 30/4/11	24750.00

(2) The 'overlap profits' are:

£ | 22,688

55.688
(33.000)
22688

Task 1.9

Mr Phone commenced trading on 1 July 2009 making up accounts to 31 May each year.

Profits are:

	£
1 July 2009 to 31 May 2010 _11 months_	22,000
Year ended 31 May 2011	18,000
Year ended 31 May 2012	30,000

(1) Using the pro forma layout provided, calculate the taxable profits for the years 2009/10 to 2011/12.

Tax year	Basis period	Taxable profits
2009/10	1/7/09 - 5/4/10 (ACTUAL)	18,000
2010/11	(FIRST 12 MONTHS) 1/7/09 - 30/6/10	23,500
2011/12	(CYB) 1/6/10 - 31/5/11	18,000

(2) The overlap profits are:

£	19,500

59,500
(40,000)
_____
19,500

Task 1.10

Mr Mug ceased trading on 31 December 2011. His overlap profits brought forward amount to £9,000. His profits for the last few periods of account were:

	£
Year ended 30 April 2009	36,000
Year ended 30 April 2010	48,000
Year ended 30 April 2011	16,000
Eight months ended 31 December 2011	4,000

Using the pro forma layout provided, calculate the taxable profits for the last three tax years of trading.

Tax year	Basis period	Taxable profits
2009/10	1/5/08 – 30/4/09	36.000
2010/11	1/5/09 – 30/4/10	48.000
2011/12	1/5/10 – 31/12/11 (20,000 -9000)	11,000

....

Task 1.11

Jackie Smith started her picture framing business on 1 May 2007. Due to falling profits she ceased to trade on 28 February 2012.

Her profits for the whole period of trading were as follows.

	£
1 May 2007 – 31 July 2008	18,000
1 August 2008 – 31 July 2009	11,700
1 August 2009 – 31 July 2010	8,640
1 August 2010 – 31 July 2011	4,800
1 August 2011 – 28 February 2012	5,100

Using the pro forma layout provided, calculate the total taxable profits for each of the tax years concerned.

Tax year	Basis period	Taxable profits
2007/08	1/5/07 - 5/4/08 11	13,200
2008/09	1/8/07 - 31/7/08 12	14,400
2009/10	1/8/08 - 31/7/09	11,700
2010/11	1/8/09 - 31/7/10	8640
2011/12	1/8/10 - 28/2/12 (4800+5100 -9600)	300
	OVERLAP (13200 +14,400 - 18,000) = 9600	

Task 1.12

Pipchin has traded for many years, making up accounts to 30 September each year. His recent results have been:

Year ended	£
30 September 2009	12,000
30 September 2010	(45,000)
30 September 2011	8,000
30 September 2012	14,000

He has received property income as follows:

	£
2009/10	10,400
2010/11	11,000
2011/12	11,000
2012/13	11,000

Using the pro forma layout provided, compute Pipchin's net income for 2009/10 to 2012/13, assuming maximum claims for loss relief are made as early as possible.

	2009/10	2010/11	2011/12	2012/13
	£	£	£	£
TRADING PROFIT	12,000	NIL	8000	14000
LOSS RELIEF			(8000)	(3600)
			—	10,400
PROPERTY INCOME	10,400	11,000	11,000	11,000
	22400	11,000	11,000	21,400
LOSS RELIEF	(22400)	(11,000)	—	—
NET INCOME	NIL	NIL	11,000	21,400

Task 1.13

True or False: an individual can restrict a claim to set a trading loss against general income in order to have enough net income to use his personal allowance.

Task 1.14

True or False: an individual must make a trading loss claim against general income in the tax year of the loss before making a claim to set the loss against general income in the preceding year.

Task 1.15

True or False: an individual can only carry a trading loss forward against trading income of the same trade.

Task 1.16

Abraham has trading profits of £12,830 for the year ended 31 December 2011.

The liability to Class 4 and Class 2 NICs for 2011/12 is:

£ | 634 | . | 45

$52 \times 2.50 = 130.00$

$(12830 - 7225) \times 9\% = 504.45$

Task 1.17

John has profits of £48,000 for the year ended 31 March 2012.

The liability to Class 4 and Class 2 NICs for 2011/12 is:

$52 \times 2.50 = 130.00$

$(42,475 - 7225) \times 9\% = 3172.50$

$(48,000 - 42,475) \times 2\% = 110.50$

$\overline{3413}$

£ | 3413 | . | 0 0

Task 1.18

Raj has accounting profits of £4,000 and trading profits of £3,500 for 2011/12.

The liability to Class 4 and Class 2 NICs for 2011/12 is:

£ | 0 | . | 0 0

Task 1.19

Zoë is a self employed author who starts in business on 6 April 2011. In the year to 5 April 2012 she had taxable trading profits of £80,000.

(1) The date by which Zoe must notify that he or she is liable to Class 2 NICs is:

31/1/13

(2) The NICs payable by Zoë for 2011/12 are:

$52 \times 2.50 = 130.00$

$(42,475 - 7225) \times 9\% = 3172.50$

$(80,000 - 42,475) \times 2\% = 750.50$

£ | 4053 | . | 0 0

Task 1.20

Graham has carried on business for many years making up accounts to 31 March each year.

The following information is relevant to his period of account to 31 March 2012:

	£
Revenue (turnover)	150,000 ✗
Cost of goods bought Box 16	25,000 ✓
Heating	1,200 —
Insurance } Box 20	560 ✓
Office costs Box 22	1,700 —
Bank charges Box 25	150 ✓
Accountancy and legal costs (£500 disallowable as relates to capital) Box 27	1,650 ✓
Goods taken for own use (market value)	750 ✗
New car (CO_2 emissions 170 g/km)	19,000 ✗

Box 42

Using this information, complete the self-employment page.

Business expenses

Read pages SEFN 7 to SEFN 9 of the *notes* to see what expenses are allowable for tax purposes.

Total expenses	Disallowable expenses
If your annual turnover was below £70,000 you may just put your total expenses in box 30	Use this column if the figures in boxes 16 to 29 include disallowable amounts

	Total expenses		Disallowable expenses
16	Cost of goods bought for resale or goods used — £ 25000 . 00	31	£ . 0 0
17	Construction industry - *payments to subcontractors* — £ . 0 0	32	£ . 0 0
18	Wages, salaries and other staff costs — £ . 0 0	33	£ . 0 0
19	Car, van and travel expenses — £ . 0 0	34	£ . 0 0
20	Rent, rates, power and insurance costs — £ 1760 . 00	35	£ . 0 0
21	Repairs and renewals of property and equipment — £ . 0 0	36	£ . 0 0
22	Phone, fax, stationery and other office costs — £ 1700 . 00	37	£ . 0 0
23	Advertising and business entertainment costs — £ . 0 0	38	£ . 0 0
24	Interest on bank and other loans — £ . 0 0	39	£ . 0 0
25	Bank, credit card and other financial charges — £ 150 . 00	40	£ . 0 0
26	Irrecoverable debts written off — £ . 0 0	41	£ . 0 0
27	Accountancy, legal and other professional fees — £ 1650 . 00	42	£ 500 . 00
28	Depreciation and loss/profit on sale of assets — £ . 0 0	43	£ . 0 0
29	Other business expenses — £ . 0 0	44	£ . 0 0
30	Total expenses in boxes 16 to 29 — £ 30260 . 00	45	Total disallowable expenses in boxes 31 to 44 — £ 500 . 00

Partnerships

Task 2.1

Fimbo and Florrie commenced in partnership on 1 January 2010. They produce accounts to 31 December each year and their profits have been as follows:

	Taxable profit £
Year ended 31 December 2010	10,000
Year ended 31 December 2011	20,000
Year ended 31 December 2012	25,000

Until 31 December 2011 Fimbo took 60% of the profits after receiving a £5,000 salary. Florrie took the remaining 40% of profits.

On 1 January 2012, Fimbo and Florrie invite Pom to join the partnership. It is agreed that Fimbo's salary will increase to £6,500 and the profits will then be split equally between the three partners.

Using the pro forma layout provided, show the division of profit for the three periods of account.

	Total £	Fimbo £	Florrie £	Pom £
12 months to 31 December 2010				
SALARY	5000	5000		
PROFITS	5000	3000	2000	
	10,000	8000	2000	
12 months to 31 December 2011				
SALARY	5000	5000		
PROFITS	15000	9000	6000	
	20,000	14000	6000	
12 months to 31 December 2012				
SALARY	6500	6500		
PROFITS	18500	6167	6167	6166
	25000	12667	6167	6166

Task 2.2

John, Paul and George began to trade as partners on 1 January 2009. The profits of the partnership are shared in the ratio 4:3:3. The accounts for recent periods have shown the following results:

	£
Period to 31 July 2009 7 MONTHS	24,300
Year to 31 July 2010	16,200
Year to 31 July 2011	14,900

(1) Using the pro forma layout provided, show the allocation of trading profits for all three periods of account.

	Total £	John £	Paul £	George £
Period ended 31 July 2009				
	24.300	9720	7290	7290
Year ended 31 July 2010				
	16200	6480	4860	4860
Year ended 31 July 2011				
	14900	5960	4470	4470

(2) Using the pro forma layout provided, calculate the taxable trading profits of John, Paul and George for all tax years.

	John £	Paul £	George £
2008/09			
1/1/09 TO 5/4/09	4166	3124	3124
2009/10			
1/1/09 TO 31/12/09	12420	9315	9315
2010/11			
1/8/09 TO 31/7/10	6480	4860	4860
2011/12			
1/8/10 TO 31/7/11	5960	4470	4470

LESS THAN 12 MONTHS

Task 2.3

Strange and his partners Pavin and Lehman had traded for many years. Strange had contributed £20,000 to the business and Pavin £10,000.

Profits were shared in the ratio of 3:2:1 after providing Strange and Pavin with salaries of £15,000 and £5,000 and interest on capital of 5%.

On 1 August 2011 the profit sharing arrangements were changed to 2:2:1 after providing only Strange with a salary of £20,000, and no further interest on capital for any of the partners.

The partnership profit for the year to 31 December 2011 was £48,000.

Using the pro forma layout provided, show the allocation of profit for the year to 31 December 2011.

	Total	Strange	Pavin	Lehman
Year ended 31 December 2011	£	£	£	£
1/1/2011 - 31/7/2011				
SALARIES	11667	8750	2917	—
INTEREST ON CAPITAL	875	583	292	—
PROFIT SHARE 3:2:1	15458	7729	5153	2576
(28,000 - 11667+875)	28,000	17062	8362	2576
1/8/2011 - 31/12/2011				
SALARY	8333	8333	—	—
PROFIT SHARE 2:2:1	11667	4667	4667	2333
(20,000 - 8333)	20,000	13000	4667	2333
TOTAL	48,000	30062	13029	4909

Task 2.4

Bob, Annie and John started their partnership on 1 June 2006 and make accounts up to 31 May each year. The accounts have always shown taxable profits.

For the period up to 31 January 2011 each partner received a salary of £15,000 per annum and the remaining profits were shared 50% to Bob and 25% each to Annie and John. There was no interest on capital or drawings.

Bob left the partnership on 1 February 2011. The profit sharing ratio, after the same salaries, changed to 50% each to Annie and John.

Profits for the year ending 31 May 2011 were £90,000.

Using the pro forma layout provided, calculate each partner's share of the profits for the year to 31 May 2011.

	Total £	Bob £	Annie £	John £
1/6/2010 – 31/1/2011				
SALARY	30,000	10,000	10,000	10,000
PROFITS	30,000	15,000	7500	7500
	60000	25000	17500	17,500
1/2/2011 TO 31/5/2011				
SALARY	10,000	—	5000	5000
PROFITS	20,000	—	10000	10000
	30,000		15,000	15,000
TOTAL PROFITS	90,000	25,000	32,500	32,500

Task 2.5

Wendy and Jayne have been in partnership as interior designers for many years, trading as Dramatic Decors.

On 1 January 2012, Wendy and Jayne admitted Paula to the partnership. From that date, partnership profits were shared 40% to each of Wendy and Jayne and 20% to Paula. The partnership continued to make up its accounts to 31 December and the trading profit for the year to 31 December 2012 was £160,000. $= 32000$

Paula had not worked for many years prior to becoming a partner in Dramatic Decors.

(1)   The share of profits taxable on Paula for 2011/12 is:

£	8000

2011/12   1/1/12 - 5/4/12 = 8000 (OVERLAP)
2012/13   1/1/12 - 31/12/12 = 32,000
                                         40,000

and for 2012/13 is:

£	32,000

and the overlap profits to carry forward are:

NICS
$(8000 - 7225) \times 9\%$
$= 69.75$

£	8000

(2)   The Class 4 National Insurance Contributions payable by Paula for 2011/12 are:

£	69.75

• •

Task 2.6

Anne Curtis and Bettina Stone have been trading in partnership selling designer dresses for many years, making up accounts to 31 December each year. They share profits equally.

The following information relates to the year to 31 December 2011:

	£
Revenue (turnover)	125,000
Cost of goods bought	(75,000)
Rental of shop	(12,000)
General administration	(1,700)
Accountancy	(650)
Goods taken for own use (market value)	1,550
New sewing machine for alterations	(1,200)

36,000

Using this information, complete page 6 of the Partnership Tax return which follows for Anne Curtis

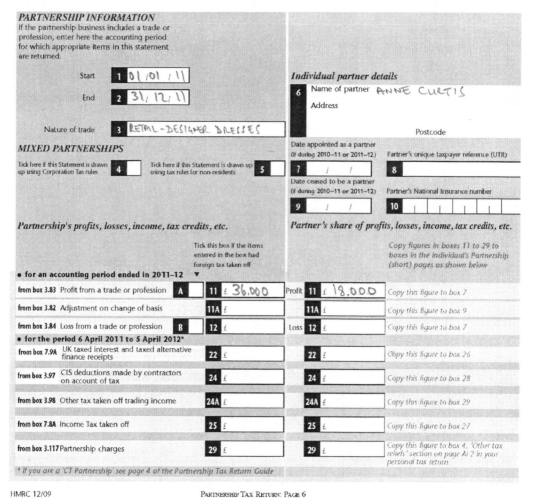

Companies

Task 3.1

Geronimo Ltd's summarised income statement (profit and loss account) for the year ended 31 March 2012 is as follows:

	£	£
Gross profit		925,940
Operating expenses		
Depreciation ADD	83,420	
Gifts (Note 1)	2,850	
Professional fees (Note 2)	14,900	
Repairs and renewals (Note 3)	42,310	
Other expenses (all allowable)	165,980	
		(309,460)
Operating profit		616,480
Income from investments		
Debenture interest (Note 4) DEDUCT	24,700	
Bank interest (Note 4)	4,800	
Dividends (Note 5)	56,000	
		85,500
		701,980
Interest payable on loans for trading purposes		(45,000)
Profit before taxation		656,980

Note 1 – Gifts

Gifts are as follows:

	£
Donation to national charity (made under the Gift Aid scheme)	1,900
Donation to local charity (Geronimo Ltd received free advertising In the charity's magazine)	50
Gifts to customers (food hampers costing £30 each)	900
	2,850

Question bank

Note 2 – Professional fees

Professional fees are as follows:

	£
Accountancy and audit fee	4,100
Legal fees in connection with the renewal of a 20-year property lease	2,400
Legal fees in connection with the issue of a debenture loan	8,400
	14,900

Note 3 – Repairs and renewals

The figure of £42,310 for repairs includes £6,200 for replacing part of a wall that was knocked down by a lorry, and £12,200 for initial repairs to an office building that was acquired during the year ended 31 March 2012. The office building was not usable until the repairs were carried out, and this fact was represented by a reduced purchase price.

Note 4

The bank interest and the debenture interest were both received on non-trade investments.

Note 5 – Dividends received

The dividends were received from other companies. The figure of £56,000 is the actual amount received.

Note 6 – Capital allowances

Capital allowances for the year have been calculated as £13,200.

Using the pro forma layout provided, calculate Geronimo Ltd's taxable trading profit for the year ended 31 March 2012.

	£	£
NET PROFIT		656,980
ADD : DEPRECIATION	83,420	
GIFTS	2800	
REPAIRS TO OFFICE	12200	98,420
		755,400
LESS : DEBENTURE	24,700	
BANK INTEREST	4800	
DIVIDENDS	56,000	
CAPITAL ALLOWANCES	13,200	(98,700)
		656,700

26

Task 3.2

The detailed income statement (profit and loss account) for Goat Ltd for the year ended 31 December 2011 is as follows:

	£	£
Revenue (turnover)		2,500,000
Cost of sales		(1,000,000)
Gross profit		1,500,000
Add: dividends received (net)	1,460	
profit on sale of shares	780	
bank interest	1,500	
		3,740
Less: debenture interest	6,750	
directors' salaries	90,000	
depreciation	150,000 ✕	
wages and salaries	220,000	
office overheads (all allowable)	400,000	
bank overdraft interest (gross)	7,000	
Gift Aid donation	1,500 ✕	
staff party	400	
customer entertainment	750 ✕	
		(876,400)
Net profit		627,340

Note

Capital allowances for the year amount to £123,000.

Using the pro forma layout provided, compute taxable trading profit for the year to 31 December 2011.

	£	£
NET PROFIT		627.340
LESS : DIVIDENDS REC.	1460	
PROFIT ON SALE	780	
BANK INTEREST	1500	
CAPITAL ALLOWANCES	123,000	
		(126.740)
		500.600
ADD: DEPRECIATION	150,000	
GIFT AID	1,500	
ENTERTAINING	750	
		152.250
TAXABLE TRADING PROFIT		652.850

Task 3.3

Righteous plc used to make its accounts up to 31 December. However, the directors decided to change the accounting date to 31 May and make up accounts for a 17-month period to 31 May 2012. The following information relates to the period of account from 1 January 2011 to 31 May 2012:

	£
Trading profit	500,000
Property business income	15,300
Capital gain on property sold on:	
1 May 2012	3,000
Gift Aid donations paid on:	
28 February 2011	15,000
31 August 2011	15,000
28 February 2012	40,000

No capital allowances are claimed.

Using the pro forma layout provided, compute taxable total profits for the accounting periods based on the above accounts.

1/1/11 — 31/12/11	JAN-DEC 2011 £	JAN-MAY 2012 £
TRADING PROFIT (500,000 × 12/17)	352,941	147,059
PROPERTY BUSINESS	10,800	4,500
CAPITAL GAIN	0	3000
LESS: GIFT AID	(30,000)	(40,000)
	333,741	114,559

Task 3.4

When a company has a period of account which exceeds 12 months, how are the following apportioned:

	Time apportioned	Period in which arises	Separate computation
Capital allowances	☐	☐	☑
Trading income	☑	☐	☐
Property income	☑	☐	☐
Interest income	☐	☑	☐
Chargeable gain	☐	☑	☐

Task 3.5

At the end of the period of account to 31 March 2011, the values of plant and machinery in Green Ltd's tax computations were as follows:

	£
Main pool	106,000
Short-life asset (spring end grinding machine)	17,500

The short-life asset was purchased on 7 August 2009 and was sold on 19 November 2011 for £5,000.

On 1 January 2012 a car costing £14,000 was acquired. The CO_2 emissions of the car were 170 g/km.

There were no other purchases or sales during the year. The company had always prepared accounts to 31 March.

Using the pro forma layout provided, calculate the capital allowances available in the year ended 31 March 2012.

Y/E 31 MARCH 2012	MAIN POOL	SHORT-LIFE ASSET	CAR	ALLOWANCES
B/F	106.000	17.500		
DISPOSAL SHORT LIFE ASSET		(5000)		
BALANCING ALLOWANCE		12.500		12.500
ADDITION 1.1.12 CAR			14.000	
WDA @ 10%			(1400)	1400
WDA @ 20%	(21,200)		12.600	21200
BALANCE C/F	84.800		12.600	35100
CAPITAL ALLOWANCES				35100

....

Task 3.6

T Ltd has four wholly owned trading subsidiaries. It had taxable total profits for the eight months to 30 November 2011 of £38,000 and had franked investment income of £4,000.

Using the pro forma layout provided, compute the corporation tax payable.

	£
TAXABLE TOTAL PROFITS 38,000 @ 26%	9880.00
AUGMENTED PROFITS 4,000 / 42,000	(2144.29)
MARGINAL RELIEF	7735.71

....

$$(1.500.000 \div 5) \times 8/12 = 200,000$$

$$(300.000 \div 5) \times 8/12 = 40,000$$

$$3/200 \times \left(200,000 - 42.000\right) \times \frac{38,000}{42.000}$$

$$158.000$$

Task 3.7

Rosemary Ltd has the following results for the ten-month period ended 31 March 2012:

	£
Taxable trading profits	600,000
Property business income	300,000
Dividends received	162,000

(1) Using the pro forma layout provided, calculate Rosemary Ltd's augmented profits.

	£
TAXABLE TRADING PROFITS	600,000
PROPERTY BUSINESS INCOME	300,000
	900,000
	~~180000~~
DIVIDENDS	1080000

(2) By filling in the shaded boxes, compute the corporation tax payable.

£

900,000   @ 26%   234000

Less:

3/200 × 1250,000 minus 1,080,000 × 900,000   2125
                  170,000   1080000

Corporation Tax payable   231875

Task 3.8

Island Ltd has two wholly owned trading subsidiaries. In order to align its accounts date with its subsidiaries, Island Ltd draws up accounts for the eight months to 31 December 2011, showing the following results.

		£
Trading profits	UPPER LIMIT 500,000 = 333.333 LOWER LIMIT 100,000 = 66,667	300,000
Chargeable gain		60,000

(1) Using the pro forma layout provided, calculate the taxable total profits.

	£
TOTAL PROFITS 300,000 + 60,000 @ 26% 3/... (500,000 - 300,000)	93600

(2) The corporation tax payable is:

£ | 93.600 | · | 00

....

Task 3.9

Basil Ltd, a company with no associated companies had the following results:

		9 months to 30.6.11
		£
Trading profits	1125,000	150,000
Chargeable gains	225,000	60,000
Dividend received (net)		9,000

(1) Using the pro forma layout provided, calculate Basil Ltd's augmented profits

		£
TRADING PROFITS		150,000
GAINS		60,000
		210,000
DIVIDENDS	9000 × 100/90	10,000
AUGMENTED PROFITS		220,000

(2) The corporation tax payable is:

£ | 43.400 | · | 00

6 MONTHS 2010 — 29,400
3 MONTHS 2011 — 14,000
43.400

Task 3.10

Pennington Ltd produced the following results:

	Year ended 30 June		
	2009	2010	2011
	£	£	£
Trading profit/(loss)	62,000	20,000	(83,000)
Interest income	1,200	600	1,200
Gift Aid donation	100	50	100

(1) Using the pro forma layout provided, compute Pennington Ltd's taxable total profits for the above accounting periods, assuming the loss relief is claimed as soon as possible.

	Year ended 30 June		
	2009	2010	2011
TRADING PROFIT	62,000	20,000	NIL
INTEREST	1200	600	1200
	63200	20,600	1200
CURRENT PERIOD REL	—	—	(1200)
	63,200	20,600	—
CARRY BACK RELIEF	—	(20,600)	—
LESS GIFT AID	(100)	—	—
TAXABLE TOTAL	63,100	NIL	NIL
UNRELIEVED GIFT AID	—	50	100

83,000
(1200)
(20,600)

(2) The trading loss available to carry forward at 30 June 2011 is:

£ 61200

Task 3.11

Ferraro Ltd has the following results.

	30.09.09	9 months to 30.6.10	Year ended 30.6.11	Year ended 30.6.12
	£	£	£	£
Trading profit (loss)	6,200	4,320	(100,000)	53,000
Bank deposit interest accrued	80	240	260	200
Rents receivable	1,420	1,440	1,600	1,500
Capital gain	–	12,680	–	–
Allowable capital loss	(5,000)	–	(9,423)	
Gift Aid donation paid (gross)	1,000	1,000	1,500	1,500

(1) Using the pro forma layout provided, compute all taxable total profits, claiming loss reliefs as early as possible.

	30.09.09	9 MONTHS To 30.6.10	YE 30.6.11	YE 30.6.12
TRADING	6200	4320	NIL	53,000
INTEREST	80	240	260	200
RENT	1420	1440	1600	1500
GAINS	—	7680	(—	—
	7700	13680	1860	54,700
CF RELIEF	—	—	(1860)	—
CB RELIEF	(1925)	(13680)	—	—
CF RELIEF	—	—	—	(53,000)
LESS GIFTAID	(1000)	—	—	(1500)
TAXABLE	4775	NIL	NIL	200

(2) The trading loss available to carry forward at 30 June 2012 is:

£ 29535

(3) The capital loss available to carry forward at 30 June 2012 is:

£ 9423

Task 3.12

True or False: a company must offset its trading loss against total profits in the loss-making period before carrying the loss back.

Task 3.13

True or False: if a company carries a trading loss forward, the loss can be set against total profits in the following accounting period.

Task 3.14

True or False: a company can set-off a capital loss against trading profits.

Task 3.15

Cranmore Ltd is a trading company manufacturing specialist engineering tools. It makes up its accounts to 31 March each year. It has no associated companies.

For the year to 31 March 2012, the company had the following results:

	£
Revenue (turnover)	525,000
Trading profit before capital allowances DEDUCT CAPITAL	405,000 −11,000
Interest received from building society deposit	3,000
Property business income from letting out part of factory	16,000
	424,000

The capital allowances have been computed to be £11,000, of which £3,000 is Annual Investment Allowance, £5,500 is writing down allowance on the main pool and £2,500 is writing down allowance on an expensive car acquired before 6 April 2009.

Using the above information, show the entries that need to be made on the Form CT600.

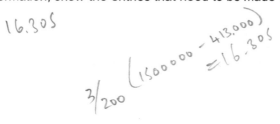

16.30S

$\frac{3}{200}$ (1500000 − 413.000) = 16.30S

Page 2
Company tax calculation

Turnover

1 Total turnover from trade or profession   **1** £ 525,000.00

Income

3 Trading and professional profits   **3** £ 394,000.00   DEDUCT CAPITAL ALLOWANCE

4 Trading losses brought forward claimed against profits   **4** £

5 Net trading and professional profits (DEDUCT CAPITAL ALLOWANCE)   box 3 minus box 4   **5** £ 394,000.00

6 Bank, building society or other interest, and profits and gains from non-trading loan relationships   **6** £ 3000.00

11 Income from UK land and buildings   **11** £ 16000.00

14 Annual profits and gains not falling under any other heading   **14** £

Chargeable gains

16 Gross chargeable gains   **16** £

17 Allowable losses including losses brought forward   **17** £

18 Net chargeable gains   box 16 minus box 17   **18** £

21 Profits before other deductions and reliefs   sum of boxes 5, 6, 11, 14 & 18   **21** £ 413,000.00

Deductions and Reliefs

24 Management expenses under S75 ICTA 1988   **24** £

30 Trading losses of this or a later accounting period under S393A ICTA 1988   **30** £

31 Put an 'X' in box 31 if amounts carried back from later accounting periods are included in box 30   **31**

32 Non-trade capital allowances   **32** £

35 Charges paid   **35** £

37 Taxable total profits   box 21 minus boxes 24, 30, 32 and 35   **37** £

Tax calculation

38 Franked investment income   **38** £ 0

39 Number of associated companies in this period   **39** 0
or

40 Associated companies in the first financial year   **40**

41 Associated companies in the second financial year   **41**

42 Put an 'X' in box 42 if the company claims to be charged at the starting rate or the small companies' rate on any part of its profits, or is claiming marginal rate relief   **42** ☒

Enter how much profit has to be charged and at what rate of tax

Financial year (yyyy)	Amount of profit	Rate of tax	Tax	
43 2011	**44** £ 413000.00	**45** 2600	**46** £ 107,380.00	p
53	**54** £	**55**	**56** £	p

   total of boxes 46 and 56   **63** £ 107,380.00 p

63 Corporation tax

64 Marginal rate relief   **64** £ 16305.00 p

65 Corporation tax net of marginal rate relief   **65** £ 91075.00 p

66 Underlying rate of corporation tax   **66** . %

67 Profits matched with non-corporate distributions   **67**

68 Tax at non-corporate distributions rate   **68** £ p

69 Tax at underlying rate on remaining profits   **69** £ p

70 Corporation tax chargeable   See note for box 70 in CT600 Guide   **70** £ 91,075.00 p

CT600 (Short) (2008) Version 2

Chargeable gains for individuals

Task 4.1

For the gain on the disposal of a capital asset to be a chargeable gain there must be a chargeable

> DISPOSAL

of a chargeable

> ASSET

by a chargeable

> PERSON

Task 4.2

Identify whether the following assets are chargeable assets or exempt assets for CGT:

Item	Chargeable	Exempt
Van	✓	☐
A plot of land	✓	☐
Car	☐	✓

Task 4.3

Romana purchased a freehold holiday cottage for £40,000. She then spent £5,000 on a new conservatory. She sold the cottage for £90,000 on 15 March 2012. Romana had not made any other disposals during 2011/12.

What is her taxable gain for 2011/12?

A £34,400

B £39,400

C £45,000

D £50,000

> 90,000
> (40,000)
> (5000)
> 45,000
> (10,600)
> 34,400

Task 4.4

Harry bought a three-acre plot of land for £150,000. He sold two acres of the land at auction for £240,000. His disposal costs were £3,000. The market value of the one remaining acre at the date of sale was £60,000.

(1) The cost of the land sold is:

£ | 120,000

$$\frac{240,000}{240,000 + 60,000} \times 150,000 = 120,000$$

(2) The gain on sale is:

£ | 117,000

```
  240,000
  (3,000)
  237.000
 (120,000)
  117,000
```

Task 4.5

In August 2011 George made chargeable gains of £20,000 and allowable losses of £3,560. He made no other disposals during 2011/12 and he is a higher rate taxpayer.

(1) George's capital gains tax liability for 2011/12 is:

£ | 1635 | . | 20

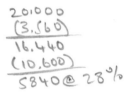

```
  20,000
  (3,560)
  16,440
 (10,600)
  5840 @ 28%
```

(2) George's capital gains tax liability is payable by:

31/1/13

Task 4.6

In November 2011, Graham made chargeable gains of £25,000 and allowable losses of £5,200. He made no other disposals during 2011/12 and he is a higher rate taxpayer.

Graham's capital gains tax liability for 2011/12 is:

£ | 2576 | . | 00

```
  25,000
  (5200)
  19800
 (10,600)
  9200  @ 28%
```

Task 4.7

Gayle made chargeable gains of £5,000 in August 2011 and £17,500 in November 2011. In July 2011 she made allowable losses of £2,000. She has unused basic rate band of £5,000 in 2011/12.

Gayle's capital gains tax liability for 2011/12 is:

£ | 2272 | . | 00

```
  5000
  17500
 (2000)
  20,500
 (10,600)
  9900 @
```

5000 @ 18% = 900
4900 @ 28% = 1372

27,000
(10,600)
16400

Task 4.8

Gerry made chargeable gains of £27,000 in December 2011. She made no other disposals in the year. Her taxable income (ie after deducting the personal allowance) for 2011/12 was £25,900.

35,000

Gerry's capital gains tax liability for 2011/12 is: *(25,900)*

9100

9100 @ 18% = 1638
7300 @ 28% = 2044
3682

£ | 3682 | . | 00

Task 4.9

Kevin made gains of £17,800 and losses of £7,000 in 2011/12. He has losses brought forward of £5,000.

The losses to carry forward to 2012/13 are:

17,800
(7,000)
10,800
10,600
200
(200)
NIL

£ | 4800

Task 4.10

Elias has the following gains and losses arising from disposals of chargeable assets:

Tax year	2009/10	2010/11	2011/12
Gains	£2,000	£4,000	£13,400
Losses	£(14,000)	£(2,000)	£(2,000)

-12,000 *+2000* *+11,400*

The maximum allowable loss carried forward to 2012/13 will be:

A   £0

B   £2,000

C   £11,200

D   £12,200

Task 4.11

Leonora purchased a picture for £5,500 and sold it in September 2011 for £7,500, incurring £300 expenses of sale.

Her chargeable gain on sale is:

7500
(300)
7200
(5500)
1700

5/3 x 7500 - 6000

A   £1,300

B   £2,000

C   £2,500

(D)   £1,700

Task 4.12

Mick purchased an antique vase for £9,000. He sold the vase in August 2011 at auction for £4,500 net of auctioneer's fees of 10%.

Mark's allowable loss is:

£ | 3500

(handwritten:)
DEEMED 6000
LESS FEES (500)
5500
(9000)
(3500)

Task 4.13

Chloe bought a necklace for £4,000. She sold it in September 2011 for £5,500.

True or False: Chloe has a chargeable gain on sale of £1,500. NIL

Task 4.14

In August 2011, John gave his daughter an asset worth £10,000. He had acquired the asset for £25,000. *(handwritten: (15,000) CAN'T BE OFFSET AGAINST BROTHER)*

In March 2012, John gave his brother an asset worth £60,000. John had acquired the asset for £15,000. *(handwritten: 60,000 – 15,000 = 45,000)*

John's chargeable gains (before the annual exempt amount) for 2011/12 are:

A £45,000

B £30,000

C £34,900

D £19,900

Task 4.15

True or False: a disposal to a connected person is at market value.

Task 4.16

Jake sold 5,000 ordinary shares for £20,000 in JKL plc on 10 August 2011. He bought 6,000 shares in JKL plc for £9,000 on 15 July 2009 and another 1,000 shares for £4,200 on 16 August 2011.

His net gain on sale is:

£ | 9800

(handwritten:)
COST
1000 @ 4200
4000 @ 6000
10200

20,000
(10,200)
9800

Task 4.17

Susan's dealings in K plc were as follows:

	No. of shares	Cost/(proceeds) £
10 February 1997	12,000	18,000
20 September 2004	Bonus issue of 1 for 4	Nil
15 March 2012	(2,000)	(8,000)

Using the pro forma layout provided, calculate the gain on sale.

Share pool

		No of shares	Cost £
10 FEB 97	ACQUISITION	12,000	18,000
20 SEP 04	BONUS	3000	—
		15,000	18,000
15 MAR 12	DISPOSAL	(2000)	(2400)
c/f		13,000	15,600

Gain on sale

	£
Proceeds	8000
Less: cost	(2400)
Gain	5600

Task 4.18

Geoff sold 10,000 of his shares in AC plc on 4 November 2011 for £60,000. The shares had been acquired as follows:

	No. of shares	Cost
		£
9 December 1997	12,000	4,400
12 October 2001 (rights issue 1:3 at £5)		
10 November 2011	2,000	11,500

Using the pro forma layout provided, calculate Geoff's gain on sale.

Share pool

		No of shares	Cost
			£
9 DEC 97	ACQUISITION	12,000	4400
12 OCT 01	RIGHTS ISSUE 1:3	4000	20,000
		16,000	24,400
4 NOV 11	DISPOSAL	(8,000)	(12,200)
	C/F	8,000	12,200

Gains on sale

	£	£
PROCEEDS ²/₁₀ x 60000	12,000	
LESS: NEXT 30 DAY ACQUISITION	(11,500)	
		500
SHARE POOL ⁸/₁₀ x 60000	48,000	
LESS COST - SHAREPOOL	(12,200)	
		35,800
TOTAL GAINS		36,300

Task 4.19

Ronald started in business as a sole trader in August 2004. He acquired a freehold shop for £80,000 and a warehouse for £150,000.

He sold his business as a going concern to Lesley in December 2011 and received £50,000 for goodwill, £90,000 for the shop and £130,000 for the warehouse. Ronald made no other chargeable gains in 2011/12 and he is a higher rate taxpayer.

Using the pro forma layout provided, compute the CGT payable by Ronald for 2011/12.

Task 4.20

True or False: the lifetime limit of gains eligible for entrepreneurs' relief for gains on or after 6 April 2011 is £10,000,000.

Task 4.21

Simon acquired 10,000 Blue Ltd shares worth £65,000 in September 1989 as a gift from his father. The father had originally acquired them as an investment in 1984 and gift relief was claimed on the gain of £15,000. Simon sold the Blue Ltd shares for £200,000 on 30 November 2011. He has no other assets for CGT purposes and made no other disposals in 2011/12.

The taxable gain arising on the sale of the Blue Ltd shares is:

£ [   ]

Task 4.22

Fran gave a factory worth £500,000 to her friend Anna on 1 June 2011. Fran had bought the factory on 1 January 1994 for £75,000 and a claim for gift relief was made. On 1 July 2012 Anna sold the factory for £520,000.

(1)   Fran's gain on her disposal is:

£ [   ]

(2)   Anna's gain on her disposal is:

£ [   ]

Task 4.23

On 6 April 1986 Edward acquired for £60,000 a small workshop where he carried on his trade as a furniture maker. On 6 August 2011 he sold the workshop for £125,000 having moved on 10 April 2011 to smaller premises which cost £123,500.

(1)   Edward's gain on the disposal before rollover relief is:

£ [   ]

(2)   Assuming rollover relief is claimed, the gain immediately chargeable is:

£ [   ]

(3)   The gain which Edward can rollover into the new premises is:

£ [   ]

ALSO   5.7

Chargeable gains for companies

Task 5.1

On 14 April 2011, Fire Ltd sold a factory for £230,000. This had originally been purchased in April 1991 for £140,000.

Indexation factor

April 1991 – April 2011   0.781

Using the pro forma layout provided calculate the chargeable gain arising on the disposal of the factory.

PROCEEDS	230 000
Allowable COST	(140,000)
UNINDEXED GAIN	90,000
INDEXATION ALLOWANCE (RESTRICTED)	(90,000)
CHARGEABLE GAIN/ALLOWABLE LOSS	NIL

Task 5.2

On 18 July 2011, Earth plc sold a warehouse for £180,000. This had been purchased in May 2002 for £100,000. Earth plc had spent £25,000 on an extension to the warehouse in August 2004.

Indexation factors

May 2002 – July 2011   0.292
August 2004 – July 2011   0.241

Using the pro forma layout provided calculate the chargeable gain arising on the disposal of the warehouse.

PROCEEDS	180,000
LESS: COST	(100,000)
NET PROCEEDS	80,000
LESS: ENHANCEMENT EXPENDITURE	(25,000)
	55,000
INDEX ALLOW ON COST	(29,200)
INDEX ALLOW ON ENHANCEMENT	(6025)
CHARGEABLE GAIN	19775

Task 5.3

On 14 November 2011, Wind plc sold two offices for £140,000. These had been part of a large office block. The whole block had cost £250,000 in August 1998 and in November 2011 the remaining offices had a market value of £320,000.

Indexation factor

August 1998 – November 2011   0.435

$$\frac{140,000}{140,000 + 320,000} \times 250,000$$

(1) The cost of the two offices disposed of is:

£ | 76087

```
140,000
(76,087)
63,913
(33 098)
30 815
```

(2) The chargeable gain arising on the disposal is:

£ | 30 815

Task 5.4

LM plc bought a painting in October 2003 for £4,500. It sold the painting at auction in September 2011 and received £7,500 after deducting the auctioneers' commission of £500. The indexation factor between October 2003 and September 2011 is 0.273.

Complete the following computation.

	£
Proceeds	8000
Disposal costs	(500)
Cost of acquisition	(4500)
Indexation allowance	(1229)
Gain	1771
Gain using chattel marginal relief	3333
Chargeable gain	1771

Gain using chattel marginal relief: $^{5}/_{3} \times (8000 - 6000)$

Task 5.5

Standring Ltd owned 20,000 shares in Smart plc acquired as follows:

5,000 shares acquired September 1991 for £10,000

1 for 5 rights acquired October 2001 at £5 per share

14,000 shares acquired August 2002 for £84,000

Standring Ltd sold 18,000 shares in January 2012 for £155,000.

Indexation factors

September 1991 – October 2001	0.327
October 2001– August 2002	0.014
August 2002 – January 2012	0.319

Using the pro forma layout provided, calculate the chargeable gain arising on the sale in January 2012.

FA 1985 pool

	NO. SHARES	COST	INDEXED COST
SEP 91 ACQUISITION	5000	10,000	10,000
INDEXED RISE OCT 01			3270
RIGHTS ISSUE OCT 01	1000	5000	5000
	6000	15,000	18,270
INDEXED RISE AUG 02			256
AUG 02 ACQUISITION	14000	84000	84,000
	20,000	99,000	102,526
INDEXED RISE JAN 12			32,706
	20,000	99,000	135,232
DISPOSAL JAN 12	(18,000)	(89100)	(121,709)
C/F	2000	9900	13,523

Gain

PROCEEDS OF SALE	155,000
LESS:-COST	(89,100)
	65,900
LESS INDEXATION (121,709 - 89100)	(32,609)
CHARGEABLE GAIN	33,291

Task 5.6

Box plc sold 11,000 shares in Crate Ltd for £78,200 on 25 May 2011. These shares had been acquired as follows.

26 May 1993	Purchased	4,000 shares for	£24,000
30 June 1994	1 for 2 bonus issue		
24 October 2001	Purchased	5,000 shares for	£27,500

Indexation factors

May 1993– October 2001   0.232
October 2001 – May 2011   0.303

Using the pro forma layout provided, calculate the gain on disposal.

FA 1985 pool

	No. SHARES	COST	INDEXED COST
26 MAY 93 ACQUISITION	4000	24,000	24,000
30 JUN 94 1:2 BONUS	2000		
OCT 01 INDEXED RISE			5.568
24 OCT 01 ACQUISITION	5000	27,500	27,500
	11,000	51,500	57068
MAY 11 INDEXED RISE			17292
	11,000	51,500	74360
25 MAY 11 DISPOSAL	(11,000)	(51,500)	(74360)
C/F	0	0	0

Gain

PROCEEDS OF SALE	78,200
LESS COST	(51,500)
	26,700
LESS : INDEXATION (74,360 - 51,500)	(22,860)
CHARGEABLE GAIN	3840

....

Task 5.7

On 23 May 2008 Del Ltd sold a freehold property for £145,000 which had cost originally £50,000 on 9 May 1995. On 15 April 2011 Del Ltd acquired the freehold of another property for £140,000. Rollover relief was claimed.

Indexation factor

May 1995 – May 2008   0.425

(1)   The gain on disposal in May 2008 was:

£ [   ]

(2)   The gain available for rollover relief is:

£ [   ]

(3)   The base cost of the property acquired in April 2011 is:

£ [   ]

....

Task 5.8

True or False: a company is entitled to an annual exempt amount.

....

Task 5.9

True or False: indexation allowance on rights issue shares runs from the date of the rights issue even though the rights issue shares are treated as having been acquired at the time of the original acquisition to which they relate.

....

Task 5.10

L plc sold a plot of land.

If L plc wishes to claim rollover relief it must acquire a new asset between:

A   The start of the previous accounting period and the end of the next accounting period

B   Three years before and three years after the date of the disposal

C   One year before and three years after the date of the disposal

D   One year before and one year after the date of the disposal

Tax administration

Task 6.1

By which date should an individual normally submit his 2011/12 self-assessment tax return if it is to be filed online?

A 31 January 2013

B 5 April 2013

C 31 October 2012

D 31 December 2012

Task 6.2

Gordon had income tax payable of £14,500 in 2010/11. His income tax payable for 2011/12 was £20,500.

How will Gordon settle his income tax payable for 2011/12?

A The full amount of £20,500 will be paid on 31 January 2013

B Payments on account of £8,750 will be made on 31 January and 31 July 2012, with the balance of £3,000 payable on 31 January 2013

C Payments on account of £10,250 will be made on 31 January and 31 July 2012 with nothing due on 31 January 2013

D Payments on account of £7,250 will be made on 31 January and 31 July 2012, with the balance of £6,000 being paid on 31 January 2013

Task 6.3

The minimum penalty as a percentage of Potential Lost Revenue for a deliberate and concealed error on a tax return where there is a prompted disclosure is:

A 100

B 50

C 35

D 15

Task 6.4

The maximum penalty as a percentage of Potential Lost Revenue for careless error for failure to notify chargeability is:

A   0

B   20

C   30

D   35

....

Task 6.5

True or False: if an individual files her 2011/12 return online on 13 April 2013, the penalty for late filing is £100.

....

Task 6.6

True or False: the penalty for failure to keep records is £3,000 per tax year or accounting period.

....

Task 6.7

An individual is required to make a payment on account on 31 July 2012 for 2011/12. The payment is actually made on 10 November 2012.

True or False: the penalty payable is 5%.

....

Task 6.8

Boscobel plc has paid corporation tax at the main rate for many years. For the year ending 31 March 2012, it had a corporation tax liability of £500,000.

Fill in the table below showing how it will pay its corporation tax liability.

Instalment	Due date	Amount due (£)
1	14 OCT 2011	125000
2	14 JAN 2012	125000
3	14 APR 2012	125000
4	14 JUL 2012	125000

....

Task 6.9

Tick whether the following statements are **True or False**.

	True	False
A company with a period of account ending on 31 March 2012 must keep its records until 31 March 2014	☐	✓
The due date for payment of CGT for 2011/12 is 31 January 2013	✓	☐
An individual who becomes chargeable to income tax in 2011/12 must notify HMRC by 31 October 2012	☐	✓
A large company will not have to pay corporation tax by instalments if it has taxable total profits not exceeding £10m and was not large in the previous accounting period	✓	☐
A company which pays corporation tax at the small profits rate must pay its corporation tax by nine months and one day after the end of its accounting period	✓	☐

Answer bank

Answer bank

Business Tax – Practice task answers

Sole traders

Task 1.1

	Revenue	Capital
Purchase of machinery		✓
Rent paid for premises	✓	
Insurance of premises	✓	
Repairs to roof of factory	✓	
New extension to shop		✓
Purchase of new car for owner		✓
Legal fees relating to purchase of new factory		✓
Payment of staff wages	✓	
Accountancy costs	✓	
Redecoration of shop	✓	

Task 1.2

Y/e 5 April 2012	AIA £	Main pool £	Mercedes car (80%) £	Allowances £
b/f		38,500		
AIA additions				
14.7.11 Furniture	23,800			
2.4.12 Machinery	31,000			
	54,800			
AIA	(54,800)			54,800
Non-AIA additions				
30.3.12 Car			18,000	
31.3.12 Car		8,000		
Disposals				
29.3.12 Machinery		(3,000)		
		43,500		
WDA @ 20%		(8,700)		8,700
WDA @ 20%			(3,600) × 80%	2,880
c/f		34,800	14,400	
Allowances				66,380

....

Task 1.3

	AIA	FYA @ 100%	Main pool	Allowances
	£	£	£	£
Y/e 5 January 2012				
AIA addition				
6.1.11 Machinery	112,000			
AIA	(100,000)			100,000
	12,000			
Transfer to main pool	(12,000)		12,000	
FYA @ 100%				
6.7.11 Low emission car		8,000		
FYA @ 100%		(8,000)		8,000
Non-AIA addition		—		
31.10.11 Car			10,500	
			22,500	
WDA @ 20%			(4,500)	4,500
	-			
c/f			18,000	
Total allowances				112,500

Answer bank

Task 1.4

	Main pool	Car (1) @ 70%	Car (2)	Car (3) 70%	Allowances
	£	£	£	£	£
Y/e 30 April 2011					
b/f	120,000	21,000	17,500		
Non-AIA FYA/addition					
10.8.10 Car				25,000	
Disposal					
10.8.10 Car		(16,000)			
Balancing allowance		5,000 × 70%			3,500
WDA @ 20%	(24,000)				24,000
WDA lower of £3,000 and					
£17,500 × 20%			(3,000)		3,000
WDA @ 10%				(2,500) × 70%	1,750
c/f	96,000		14,500	22,500	
Allowances					32,250

··

Task 1.5

In order to decide whether a trade is being carried on the following 'badges of trade' need to be considered:

(a) *Subject matter.* When people engage in trade, they frequently do so by purchasing and re-selling objects with a view to making a profit. Objects bought for this purpose are often not the type of objects that would be bought for investment or enjoyment. This means that the subject matter of a transaction will very often indicate whether a trade is being carried on or not.

(b) *Length of ownership.* A short period of ownership is an indication of an intention to trade in a commodity.

(c) *Frequency of transactions.* Where the same type of article is repeatedly bought and sold, it will normally suggest that there is trading in that article.

(d) *Supplementary work* on or in connection with the property sold, eg modification, processing, packaging, or renovating the item sold suggests the carrying on of a trade.

(e) *Acquisition of asset.* If goods are acquired deliberately, trading may be indicated. If goods are acquired by gift or inheritance, their later sale is unlikely to constitute trading.

(f) *Profit motive.* This is usually the most important consideration though its absence does not prevent a trade being carried on if, in fact, the operation is run on commercial lines and a profit does result.

These *badges of trade* are only general indications and, in each case, all the facts must be considered before any decision can be made.

··

Task 1.6

	£	£
Profits per accounts		5,300
Add: salary paid to Mr Jelly (N1)	260	
motor expenses (N2) (£350 × 1/7)	50	
stockroom extension (N3)	101	
increase in general provision	200	
donations (N2)	10	
entertaining (N4)	90	
gifts (N5)	70	
depreciation	600	
		1,381
Taxable trading profit		6,681

Notes

(1) Appropriation of profit.
(2) Not expenditure incurred wholly and exclusively for the purpose of trade.
(3) Capital items.
(4) Entertaining expenses specifically disallowed.
(5) Gifts of alcohol specifically disallowed.

···

Task 1.7

	£	£
Net profit per accounts		19,000
Add: market value of goods taken for own use	50	
depreciation	4,000	
legal expenses (N1)	400	
entertaining (N2)	275	
		4,725
Less: decrease in impaired loss provision		(30)
Taxable trading profits		23,695

Notes

(1) Legal expenses are disallowed as they relate to a capital item.

(2) Staff entertaining is allowable. Other types of entertaining are specifically disallowable.

••

Task 1.8

(1) *Taxable profits*

Tax year	Basis period	Taxable profits
		£
2009/10	$(1.1.10 - 5.4.10) \times {}^3/_{16}$ £33,000 =	6,188
2010/11	$(6.4.10 - 5.4.11) \times {}^{12}/_{16}$ £33,000 =	24,750
2011/12	$(1.5.10 - 30.4.11) \times {}^{12}/_{16}$ £33,000 =	24,750

(2) *Overlap profits*

The profits taxed twice are those for the period 1 May 2010 to 5 April 2011:

${}^{11}/_{16} \times$ £33,000 = **£22,688**

••

Task 1.9

(1)

Tax year	Basis period	Taxable profits
2009/10:	Actual	£
	1 July 2009 to 5 April 2010	
	(9/11 × £22,000)	18,000
2010/11:	First 12 months	
	1 July 2009 to 30 June 2010	
	£22,000 + (1/12 × £18,000)	23,500
2011/12:	(CYB)	
	Year ended 31 May 2011	18,000

(2)

	£
Overlap period is 1 July 2009 to 5 April 2010	18,000
and 1 June 2010 to 30 June 2010	
(1/12 × £18,000)	1,500
	19,500

∙∙∙

Task 1.10

Tax year	Basis period	Taxable profits £
2009/10	Year ended 30 April 2009	36,000
2010/11	Year ended 30 April 2010	48,000
2011/12	1 May 2010 to 31 December 2011 (16,000 + 4,000)	20,000
	Less: overlap relief	(9,000)
		11,000

∙∙∙

Task 1.11

Tax year	Basis period	Taxable profits £
2007/08	First year – 1.5.07 to 5.4.08	
	11/15 × £18,000	13,200 ✓
2008/09	Second year 12 months to 31.7.08 (1.8.07 – 31.7.08)	
	12/15 × £18,000	14,400 ✓
2009/10	Third year y/e 31.7.09	11,700 ✓
2010/11	y/e 31.7.10	8,640 ✓
2011/12		
	y/e 31.7.11	4,800
	p/e 28.2.12	5,100
		9,900
	Less: overlap profits	(9,600)
		300 ✓

Overlap profits

Overlap period is 1 August 2007 to 5 April 2008, ie 8/15 × £18,000 = £9,600 ✓

Task 1.12

		2009/10		2010/11		2011/12		2012/113
		£		£		£		£
Trading profits		12,000		NIL		8,000		14,000
Loss relief					(3)	(8,000)	(4)	(3,600)
						–		10,400
Property income		10,400		11,000		11,000		11,000
		22,400		11,000				
Loss relief	(1)	(22,400)	(2)	(11,000)				
Net income		–		–		11,000		21,400

Loss Memo		£
Loss in 2010/11		45,000
Relief: 2009/10	(1)	(22,400)
Relief: 2010/11	(2)	(11,000)
c/f		11,600
Relief: 2011/12	(3)	(8,000)
		3,600
Relief: 2012/13	(4)	(3,600)
		–

Task 1.13

False

An individual cannot restrict a claim to set a trading loss against general income in order to have enough net income to use his personal allowance – the loss must be set-off as far as possible even if this means that the personal allowance is not available.

Task 1.14

False

An individual does not have to make a trading loss claim against general income in the tax year of the loss before making a claim to set the loss against general income in the preceding year – a claim can be made for either year or both years.

Task 1.15

True

An individual can only carry a trading loss forward against trading income of the same trade.

....

Task 1.16

	£
Profits	12,830
Less: lower profits limit	(7,225)
Excess	5,605

Class 4 NICs (9% × £5,605)	= £504.45
Class 2 NICs = £2.50 × 52	= £130.00
Total NICs £(504.45 + 130.00)	= **£634.45**

....

Task 1.17

	£
Upper profits limit	42,475
Less: lower profits limit	(7,225)
Excess	35,250

	£
Class 4 NICs (9% × £35,250)	3,172.50
+ 2% × £(48,000 – 42,475)	110.50
	3,283.00

Class 2 NICs = £2.50 × 52	= £130.00
Total NICs £(3,283.00 + 130.00)	= **£3,413.00**

....

Task 1.18

£0.00

As Raj's trading profits are below the lower profits limit, there is no liability to Class 4 NICs. He is also excepted from payment of Class 2 NICs because his accounting profits are below the small earnings exception limit.

....

Task 1.19

(1) **31 January 2013**. A self-employed person must notify HMRC that he or she is liable to Class 2 NICs by 31 January following the end of the tax year in which he or she becomes self-employed.

(2) Class 2 = £2.50 × 52 = £130.00

		£
Class4	£(42,475 – 7,225) × 9% (main)	3,172.50
	£(80,000 – 42,475) × 2% (additional)	750.50
		3,923.00

Total NICs £(3,923.00 + 130.00) = **£4,053.00**

....

Task 1.20

Box 16	£25000.00
Box 20	£1760.00
Box 22	£1700.00
Box 25	£150.00
Box 27	£1650.00
Box 30	£30260.00
Box 42	£500.00
Box 45	£500.00

....

Partnerships

Task 2.1

	Total	Fimbo	Florrie	Pom
	£	£	£	£
12 months to 31 December 2010				
Salary	5,000	5,000		
Balance 60:40	5,000	3,000	2,000	
	10,000	8,000	2,000	
12 months to 31 December 2011				
Salary	5,000	5,000		
Balance 60:40	15,000	9,000	6,000	
	20,000	14,000	6,000	
12 months to 31 December 2012				
Salary	6,500	6,500		
Balance 1:1:1	18,500	6,167	6,167	6,166
	25,000	12,667	6,167	6,166

....

Task 2.2

(1) Allocation of profits

	Total	John	Paul	George
	£	£	£	£
Period ended 31 July 2009				
4:3:3	24,300	9,720	7,290	7,290
Year ended 31 July 2010				
4:3:3	16,200	6,480	4,860	4,860
Year ended 31 July 2011				
4:3:3	14,900	5,960	4,470	4,470

(2)   *Taxable profits*

	John £	Paul £	George £
2008/09			
1 January 2009 – 5 April 2009			
3/7 × £(9,720/7,290/7,290)	4,166	3,124	3,124
2009/10			
(1 January 2009 to 31 December 2009)			
1 January 2009 to 31 July 2009	9,720	7,290	7,290
1 August 2009 to 31 December 2009			
5/12 × £(6,480/4,860/4,860)	2,700	2,025	2,025
	12,420	9,315	9,315
2010/11			
Year ended 31 July 2010	6,480	4,860	4,860
2011/12			
Year ended 31 July 2011	5,960	4,470	4,470

Task 2.3

Profit allocation

Year ended 31 December 2011	Total £	Strange £	Pavin £	Lehman £
1 January 2011 – 31 July 2011				
Interest on capital				
£1,000/500 × 7/12	875	583	292	
Salaries				
£15,000/5,000 × 7/12	11,667	8,750	2,917	
	12,542			
3:2:1 (balance)	15,458	7,729	5,153	2,576
£48,000 × 7/12	28,000	17,062	8,362	2,576
1 August 2011 – 31 December 2011				
Salary (£20,000 × 5/12)	8,333	8,333		
2:2:1 (balance)	11,667	4,667	4,667	2,333
£48,000 × 5/12	20,000	13,000	4,667	2,333
Total	48,000	30,062	13,029	4,909

Answer bank

Task 2.4

Y/e 31.5.11

	Total £	Bob £	Annie £	John £
1.6.10 – 31.1.11				
Salaries				
£15,000 × 8/12	30,000	10,000	10,000	10,000
Balance 50:25:25	30,000	15,000	7,500	7,500
£90,000 × 8/12	60,000	25,000	17,500	17,500
1.2.11 – 31.5.11				
Salaries				
£15,000 × 4/12	10,000	n/a	5,000	5,000
Balance 50:50	20,000	n/a	10,000	10,000
£90,000 × 4/12	30,000	n/a	15,000	15,000
Totals	90,000	25,000	32,500	32,500

Task 2.5

(1) Share of profits for y/e 31.12.12 is £160,000 × 20% = £32,000

2011/12

1.1.12 to 5.4.12

3/12 × £32,000 = **£8,000**

2012/13

1.1.12 to 31.12.12 = **£32,000**

Overlap period is 1.1.12 to 5.4.12 so overlap profits are **£8,000**.

(2) Class 4 NICs for 2011/12

£(8,000 – 7,225) = £775 × 9% = **£69.75**

Task 2.6

Working:

Tax adjusted trading profit for the partnership is:

	£
Revenue (turnover)	125,000
Cost of goods	(75,000)
Rental	(12,000)
Admin	(1,700)
Accountancy	(650)
Goods for own use	1,550
AIA on sewing machine	(1,200)
	36,000

Page 6	
Box 1	01.01.11
Box 2	31.12.11
Box 3	Retail – designer dresses
Box 11	36000.00
Box 6	Anne Curtis
Box 11	18000.00

....

Companies

Task 3.1

	£	£
Profit per accounts		656,980
Add: depreciation	83,420	
Gift Aid donation	1,900	
gifts to customers	900	
repairs	12,200	
		98,420
Less: debenture interest	24,700	
bank interest	4,800	
dividends	56,000	
capital allowances	13,200	
		(98,700)
Taxable trading profit		656,700

Notes

(1) The costs of renewing a short lease and of obtaining loan finance for trading purposes are allowable.

(2) The replacement of the wall is allowable since the whole structure is not being replaced. The repairs to the office building are not allowable, being capital in nature, as the building was not in a usable state when purchased and this was reflected in the purchase price.

Task 3.2

Taxable trading profits

	£	£
Net profit per accounts		627,340
Less: dividends received	1,460	
profit on the sale of shares	780	
bank interest	1,500	
capital allowances	123,000	
		(126,740)
		500,600
Add: depreciation	150,000	
Gift Aid donation	1,500	
entertaining customers	750	
		152,250
Taxable trading profit		652,850

Task 3.3

	Year to 31 December 2011 £	Five months to 31 May 2012 £
Trading profits (12:5)	352,941	147,059
Property business income (12:5)	10,800	4,500
Chargeable gain	–	3,000
	363,741	154,559
Gift Aid donation paid	(30,000)	(40,000)
Taxable total profits	333,741	114,559

Tutor's notes

(1) Trading profits are time apportioned.

(2) Property business income is time apportioned.

(3) Chargeable gains are allocated to the period in which they are realised.

(4) Gift Aid donations are allocated to the period in which they are paid.

Answer bank

Task 3.4

	Time apportioned	Period in which arises	Separate computation
Capital allowances			✓
Trading income	✓		
Property income	✓		
Interest income		✓	
Chargeable gain		✓	

Task 3.5

	Main pool £	Special rate pool £	SLA £	Allowances £
Y/e 31 March 2012				
b/f	106,000		17,500	
Disposals			(5,000)	
Balancing allowance			12,500	12,500
Addition		14,000		
WDA @ 20%/10%	(21,200)	(1,400)		1,400
c/f				21,200
Allowances				
	84,800	12,600		35,100

74

Task 3.6

There are five associated companies so the lower limit in this eight-month period is £40,000. The upper limit is £200,000.

Therefore, marginal relief applies (FY11).

	£
£38,000 × 26%	9,880.00
Less: £(200,000 – 42,000) $\frac{38,000}{42,000} \times \frac{3}{200}$	(2,144.29)
Corporation tax payable	7,735.71

Task 3.7

(1)

	£
Trading profits	600,000
Property business income	300,000
Taxable total profits	900,000
Dividends received × 100/90	180,000
Augmented profits	1,080,000

(2) Upper limit: £1,500,000 × 10/12 = £1,250,000

Lower limit: £300,000 × 10/12 = £250,000

Marginal relief applies

		£
900,000 @ 26%		234,000.00
Less:		
3/200 × 1,250,000 minus 1,080,000 × $\frac{900,000}{1,080,000}$		2,124.99
Corporation Tax payable		231,875.01

Task 3.8

(1)

	£
Trading profits	300,000
Chargeable gain	60,000
Taxable total profits/augmented profits	360,000

(2)

Upper limit $\dfrac{1,500,000}{3} \times 8/12 = £333,333$

As augmented profits are above the upper limit the main rate of tax (for FY11) applies:

$£360,000 \times 26\% = \underline{\textbf{£93,600.00}}$

··

Task 3.9

(1)

	9 months to 30 June 2011
	£
Trading profits	150,000
Chargeable gains	60,000
Taxable total profits	210,000
Dividends received × 100/90	10,000
Augmented profits	220,000

(2)

Upper limit: $1,500,000 \times 9/12 = 1,125,000$

Lower limit: $300,000 \times 9/12 = 225,000$

SPR applies

FY10 : $£210,000 \times 6/9 \times 21\%$ = 29,400.00

FY11 : $£210,000 \times 3/9 \times 20\%$ = 14,000.00

Total corporation tax payable: = **£43,400.00**

··

Task 3.10

(1)

	Year ended 30 June		
	2009	*2010*	*2011*
	£	£	£
Trading profits	62,000	20,000	–
Interest	1,200	600	1,200
	63,200	20,600	1,200
Current period loss relief	–	–	(1,200)
Carry back loss relief		(20,600)	
	63,200	–	–
Gift Aid donation	(100)		
Taxable total profits	63,100	–	–

(2) *Loss carried forward*

	£	£
Year ended 30 June 2011		83,000
Current period loss relief	(1,200)	
Carry back loss relief (12m)	(20,600)	
		(21,800)
Loss carried forward		**61,200**

Task 3.11

(1)

	12m to 30.09.09 £	9m to 30.6.10 £	12m to 30.6.11 £	12m to 30.6.12 £
Trading profits	6,200	4,320	0	53,000
Loss relief b/fwd				(53,000)
Interest	80	240	260	200
Property business income	1,420	1,440	1,600	1,500
Chargeable gain (12,680 – 5,000)	0	7,680	0	
	7,700	13,680	1,860	1,700
Less: current period			(1,860)	
	7,700	13,680	0	1,700
Less: carry back	(1,925)	(13,680)		
Less: Gift Aid donations	(1,000)	(0)	(0)	(1,500)
Taxable total profits	4,775	0	0	200

Tutor's note. The loss can be carried back to set against profits arising in the previous 12 months. This means that the set-off in the y/e 30.09.09 is restricted to 3/12 × £7,700 = £1,925.

(2) *Trading loss carried forward*

	£
Loss of y/e 30.6.11	100,000
Less used y/e 30.6.11	(1,860)
	98,140
Less used 9m/e 30.6.10	(13,680)
	84,460
Less used y/e 30.09.09	(1,925)
c/f	82,535
Less used y/e 30.06.12	(53,000)
Loss to carry forward	**29,535**

(3) The allowable capital loss of **£9,423** during the year ended 30 June 2011 is carried forward against future chargeable gains.

● ●

Task 3.12

True

A company must offset its trading loss against total profits in the loss-making period before carrying the loss back.

● ●

Task 3.13

False

If a company carries a trading loss forward, the loss can only be set against trading profits from the same trade.

● ●

Task 3.14

False

A company can set-off a capital loss against capital gains only.

● ●

Task 3.15

Total turnover (box 1): £525000.00

Taxable trading profits (box 3): £394000.00

Net trading profits (box 5): £394000.00

Interest (box 6): £3000.00

Property business income (box 11): £16000.00

Profits (box 21): £413000.00

Taxable total profits (box 37): £413000.00

Franked investment income (box 38): £0

Associated companies (box 39): 0

Marginal relief (box 42): X

Financial year (box 43): 2011

Amount of profit (box 44): £413000.00

Rate of tax (box 45): 26.00

Tax (box 46): £107380.00

Corporation tax (box 63): £107380.00

Marginal rate relief (box 64): £16305.00

Corporation tax net of marginal rate relief (box 65): £91075.00

Corporation tax chargeable (box 70): £91075.00

Chargeable gains for individuals

Task 4.1

For the gain on the disposal of a capital asset to be a chargeable gain there must be a chargeable **disposal** of a chargeable **asset** by a chargeable **person**.

···

Task 4.2

Item	Chargeable	Exempt
Van	✓	
A plot of land	✓	
Car		✓

···

Task 4.3

A

	£
Proceeds of sale	90,000
Less: cost	(40,000)
Less: enhancement expenditure	(5,000)
Chargeable gain	45,000
Less: annual exempt amount	(10,600)
Taxable gain	34,400

···

Task 4.4

(1) The cost of the land being sold is:

$$\frac{240{,}000}{240{,}000 + 60{,}000} \times £150{,}000 = £120{,}000$$

(2)

	£
Disposal proceeds	240,000
Less: disposal costs	(3,000)
Net proceeds	237,000
Less: cost	(120,000)
Chargeable gain	**117,000**

···

Task 4.5

(1)

	£
Chargeable gains	20,000
Less: allowable losses	(3,560)
Net chargeable gains	16,440
Less: annual exempt amount	(10,600)
Taxable gains	5,840
CGT @ 28%	**£1,635.20**

(2) **31 January 2013**

....

Task 4.6

	£
Chargeable gains	25,000
Less allowable losses	(5,200)
Net chargeable gains	19,800
Less annual exempt amount	(10,600)
Taxable gains	9,200

CGT @ 28% = **£2,576.00**

....

Task 4.7

	£
Chargeable gains	22,500
Less allowable losses	(2,000)
Net chargeable gains	20,500
Less annual exempt amount	(10,600)
Taxable gains	9,900

CGT payable

	£
£5,000 @ 18%	900.00
£4,900 @ 28%	1,372.00
	2,272.00

....

Task 4.8

	£
Chargeable gains	27,000
Less annual exempt amount	(10,600)
Taxable gains	16,400
CGT	£
£9,100 (W) @ 18%	1,638.00
£7,300 @ 28%	2,044.00
	3,682.00

(W) Unused basic rate band is £35,000 - £25,900 = £9,100

....

Task 4.9

	£
Gains	17,800
Losses	(7,000)
	10,800
Losses b/f (10,800 – 10,600)	(200)
	10,600
Less: annual exempt amount	(10,600)
Taxable gains	NIL
Losses c/f (5,000 – 200) =	**£4,800**

....

Answer bank

Task 4.10

C

Tax year	2009/10	2010/11	2011/12
	£	£	£
Gains	2,000	4,000	13,400
Losses	(14,000)	(2,000)	(2,000)
Net gain/(loss)	(12,000)	2,000	11,400
Less: loss b/f	(0)	0	(800)
Less: annual exempt amount	0	(2,000)	(10,600)
Chargeable gain	0	0	0
Loss c/f	(12,000)	(12,000)	(11,200)

The use of the loss brought forward in 2011/12 is restricted to the amount of the annual exempt amount.

....

Task 4.11

D

	£
Gross proceeds	7,500
Less: costs of sale	(300)
Net proceeds	7,200
Less: cost	(5,500)
Chargeable gain	1,700
Gain cannot exceed 5/3 × £(7,500 – 6,000)	2,500
So actual gain applies	£1,700

....

Task 4.12

	£
Deemed proceeds	6,000
Less: costs of sale £(4,500 × 100/90) = £5,000 × 10%	(500)
Net proceeds	5,500
Less: cost	(9,000)
Allowable loss	(3,500)

....

Task 4.13

False

The proceeds are less than £6,000 so the gain is exempt.

···

Task 4.14

A

The gain on the disposal to John's brother is £(60,000 – 15,000) = £45,000. The loss on the disposal to John's daughter can only be set against disposals to that connected person.

···

Task 4.15

True

Disposals to connected persons are at market value.

···

Task 4.16

Match acquisition in next 30 days first

	£
Proceeds of sale £20,000 × 1/5	4,000
Less: cost	(4,200)
Loss	(200)

Then match with share pool

	£
Proceeds of sale £20,000 × 4/5	16,000
Less: cost £9,000 × 4/6	(6,000)
Gain	10,000
Net gain £(10,000 – 200)	**9,800**

···

Answer bank

Task 4.17

Share pool

	No of shares	Cost £
10 February 1997	12,000	18,000
20 September 2004 Bonus 1:4	3,000	–
	15,000	18,000
15 March 2012 Disposal	(2,000)	(2,400)
c/f	13,000	15,600

	£
Proceeds	8,000
Less: cost	(2,400)
Gain	5,600

....

Task 4.18

Share pool

	No of shares	Cost £
9 December 1997: purchase	12,000	4,400
12 October 2001 Rights 1:3@ £5	4,000	20,000
	16,000	24,400
4 November 2011 Disposal	(8,000)	(12,200)
	8,000	12,200

	£	Gains/(losses) £
Next 30 days		
Proceeds $\frac{2,000}{10,000} \times £60,000$	12,000	
Less: cost	(11,500)	
		500
Share pool		
Proceeds $\frac{8,000}{10,000} \times £60,000$	48,000	
Less: cost	(12,200)	
		35,800
Total gains		36,300

....

Task 4.19

	£	£
Proceeds of goodwill	50,000	
Less: cost	(nil)	50,000
Proceeds of shop	90,000	
Less: cost	(80,000)	10,000
Proceeds of warehouse	130,000	
Less: cost	(150,000)	(20,000)
Net gains eligible for entrepreneurs' relief		40,000
Less: annual exempt amount		(10,600)
Taxable gains		29,400
CGT on £29,400 @ 10%		2,940.00

....

Task 4.20

True

The lifetime limit of gains eligible for entrepreneurs' relief is £10,000,000.

....

Task 4.21

	£	£
Proceeds		200,000
Less: cost	65,000	
Less: gain rolled over	(15,000)	
		(50,000)
Chargeable gain		150,000
Less: annual exempt amount		(10,600)
Taxable gain		**139,400**

....

Task 4.22

(1) Fran's gain

	£
Proceeds (MV) June 2011	500,000
Less: cost	(75,000)
Gain	425,000
Less: gift relief	(425,000)
Gain left in charge	**0**

(2) Anna's gain

	£	£
Proceeds July 2012		520,000
Cost (MV)	500,000	
Less: gift relief gain (from part a)	(425,000)	
Base cost		(75,000)
Chargeable gain		**445,000**

....

Task 4.23

(1)

	£
Proceeds	125,000
Less: cost	(60,000)
Gain	**65,000**

(2)

	£
Proceeds	125,000
Less: amount invested in new premises	(123,500)
Gain immediately chargeable	**1,500**

(3)

	£
Gain	65,000
Less: immediately chargeable	(1,500)
Gain rolled-over against new premises	**63,500**

....

Chargeable gains for companies

Task 5.1

	£
Proceeds	230,000
Less: cost	(140,000)
	90,000
Less: indexation allowance 0.781 × £140,000 (restricted)	(90,000)
Chargeable gain/allowable loss	Nil

Task 5.2

	£
Proceeds	180,000
Less: cost	(100,000)
enhancement expenditure	(25,000)
	55,000
Less: indexation allowance on cost 0.292 × £100,000	(29,200)
Indexation allowance on enhancement 0.241 × £25,000	(6,025)
Chargeable gain	19,775

Task 5.3

(1) $£250,000 \times \dfrac{140,000}{140,000 + 320,000} = \textbf{£76,087}$

(2)

	£
Proceeds	140,000
Less: cost	
$£250,000 \times \dfrac{140,000}{140,000 + 320,000}$	(76,087)
	63,913
Less: IA	
0.435 × £76,087	(33,098)
Chargeable gain	**30,815**

Task 5.4

	£
Proceeds	8,000
Disposal costs	500
Cost of acquisition	4,500
Indexation allowance (4,500 x 0.273)	1,229
Gain	1,771
Gain using chattel marginal relief (5/3 (8,000 – 6,000)	3,333
Chargeable gain (lower of actual gain and marginal relief)	1,771

....

Task 5.5

FA 1985 pool	No of shares	Original cost	Indexed cost
September 1991		£	£
Acquisition	5,000	10,000	10,000
October 2001			
Indexed rise 0.327 × £10,000			3,270
Rights 1:5 @ £5	1,000	5,000	5,000
	6,000	15,000	18,270
August 2002			
Indexed rise 0.014 × £18,270			256
Acquisition	14,000	84,000	84,000
	20,000	99,000	102,526
January 2012			
Indexed rise 0.319 × £102,526			32,706
			135,232
Sale (99,000/135,232 × 18000/20,000)	(18,000)	(89,100)	(121,709)
c/f	2,000	9,900	13,523

Gain

	£
Proceeds	155,000
Less: cost	(89,100)
	65,900
Less: indexation allowance £(121,709 – 89,100)	(32,609)
Chargeable gain	33,291

....

Task 5.6

FA 1985 pool

	No.	Cost	Indexed cost
		£	£
26.5.93			
Acquisition	4,000	24,000	24,000
30.6.94 Bonus issue	2,000		
24.10.01			
IA 0.232 × £24,000			5,568
			29,568
Acquisition	5,000	27,500	27,500
c/f	11,000	51,500	57,068
22.5.11			
IA 0.303 × £57,068			17,292
			74,360
Disposal	(11,000)	(51,500)	(74,360)
c/f	Nil	Nil	Nil

	£
Proceeds	78,200
Less: cost	(51,500)
	26,700
Less: indexation allowance £(74,360 – 51,500)	(22,860)
Gain	3,840

....

Task 5.7

(1)

		£
Proceeds		145,000
Less: cost		(50,000)
		95,000
Less: indexation allowance 0.425 × £50,000		(21,250)
Chargeable gain		**73,750**

(2)

	£
Gain	73,750
Less: chargeable in 2008	
Proceeds not reinvested = £(145,000 – 140,000)	(5,000)
Gain available for rollover relief	**68,750**

(3)

	£
Cost of new property	140,000
Less: gain rolled over	(68,750)
Base cost of new property	**71,250**

Task 5.8

False

Individuals are entitled to an annual exempt amount but not companies.

Task 5.9

True

Indexation allowance on rights issue shares runs from the date of the rights issue even though the rights issue shares are treated as having been acquired at the time of the original acquisition to which they relate.

Task 5.10

C

If L plc wishes to claim rollover relief it must acquire a new asset between one year before and three years after the date of the disposal.

Tax administration

Task 6.1

A

31 January 2013

....

Task 6.2

D

Payments on account of £7,250 will be made on 31 January and 31 July 2012, with the balance of £6,000 being paid on 31 January 2013.

....

Task 6.3

B

50%

....

Task 6.4

C

30%

....

Task 6.5

True

If an individual files her 2011/12 return online on 13 April 2013, the penalty for late filing is £100 as the return is filed less than 3 months after the due filing date.

....

Task 6.6

True

The penalty for failure to keep records is £3,000 per tax year or accounting period.

....

Task 6.7

False

Penalties for late payment do not apply to payments on account.

Task 6.8

Instalment	Due date	Amount due (£)
1	14 October 2011	125,000
2	14 January 2012	125,000
3	14 April 2012	125,000
4	14 July 2012	125,000

Task 6.9

	True	False
A company with a period of account ending on 31 March 2012 must keep its records until 31 March 2014		✓ (until 31 March 2018)
The due date for payment of CGT for 2011/12 is 31 January 2013	✓	
An individual who becomes chargeable to income tax in 2011/12 must notify HMRC by 31 October 2012		✓ (by 5 October 2012)
A large company will not have to pay corporation tax by instalments if it has taxable total profits not exceeding £10m and was not large in the previous accounting period	✓	
A company which pays corporation tax at the small profits rate must pay its corporation tax by nine months and one day after the end of its accounting period	✓	

SAMPLE ASSESSMENT
BUSINESS TAX

Time allowed: 2 hours

SAMPLE ASSESSMENT

Section 1

Task 1.1

For the following, tick if they are revenue or capital based.

	Revenue	Capital
Motor car	☐	☑
Rent	☑	☐
Repairs	☑	☐

Task 1.2

Zhang is a sole trader and has the following income statement (profit and loss account):

	£	£
Revenue (turnover)		1,210,210
Cost of sales		(808,480)
Gross profit		401,730
Wages and salaries	125,778	
Rent, rates and insurance	59,221	
Repairs to plant	8,215	
Advertising and entertaining	19,077	
Accountancy and legal costs	5,710	
Motor expenses	53,018	
Telephone and office costs	14,017	
Depreciation	28,019	
Other expenses	92,460	(405,515)
Loss		(3,785)

NET PROFIT   (3785)

ADD. PERSONAL SALARY   30,000
        WINE   2250
        MOTOR   5700
        GOLF   220
        DEPRECIATION   28019   66189
                                              62404
LESS. CAPITAL ALLOW   (9878)
ADJUSTED   TRADING PROFITS   52526

Notes include:

(1) Wages and salaries include: £

    Zhang   30,000 ✗

    Zhang's wife, who works in the marketing department   18,000

(2) Advertising and entertaining includes: £

    Gifts to customers:

    Bottles of wine costing £15 each   2,250 ✗

    Diaries carrying the business's logo, costing £10 each   400

    Staff Christmas party for 20 employees   1,485

(3) Motor expenses include expenses relating to: £

    Delivery vans   10,403

    Sales manager's car   6,915

    Zhang's car which is only used for private mileage   5,700 ✗

(4) Other expenses include: £

    Cost of staff training   3,550

    Subscription to a golf club for Mr Zhang   220 ✗

(5) Capital allowances have already been calculated at £9,878

Calculate the adjusted trading profit for Zhang starting with the net loss figure of £(3,785).

Task 1.3

Alan started trading on 1 February 2010. He makes up his accounts to 31 December each year. The profits were calculated at:

	£
Period to 31 December 2010	33,000
Year to 31 December 2011	40,500
Year to 31 December 2012	45,000

(1) The tax year in which he started trading was:

    (a) 2008/09

    (b) 2009/10   1/2/10 - 5/4/10

    (c) 2010/11   1/2/10 - 31/1/11

    (d) 2011/12   1/1/11 - 31/12/11

(2)   His taxable profits in his first tax year of trading were:

   (a) £2,750

   (b) £3,000

   (c) £5,500

   (d) £6,000

(3)   His taxable profits in his second tax year of trading were:

   (a) £33,000

   (b) £36,375

   (c) £40,500

   (d) £45,000

33,000
+   3375
   36375

(4)   His overlap profits were   £   [9375]

....

Task 1.4

True or false: a trading loss made by a company can only be offset against trading profits from the same trade when carrying the loss forward

....

Task 1.5

Adam and Barrie have been in partnership for many years, making up their accounts to 31 December each year. Their profit sharing ratio was 2:1 respectively.

On 1 May 2011, Charlie joined the partnership and the profit sharing ratio was changed to 3:2:1 for Adam, Barrie and Charlie.

For the year ended 31 December 2011, the trading profit was £90,000.

The division of profit would be calculated as:

	TOTAL £	ADAM £	BARRIE £	CHARLIE £
Period to: Date 30/4/11	A 30,000	B 20,000	C 10,000	

Options:

A = 90,000; 45,000; 30,000; 22,500

B = 60,000; 30,000; 20,000; 15,000; 45,000; 22,500; 15,000; 11,250

C = 45,000; 30,000; 15,000; 10,000; 7,500; 22,500; 11,250; 5,625

	TOTAL £	ADAM £	BARRIE £	CHARLIE £
Period to: Date 31/12/11	D 60,000	E 30,000	F 20,000	G 10,000

Options:

D = 90,000; 45,000; 60,000; 67,500

E = 45,000; 22,500; 30,000; 33,750; 15,000; 20,000

F = 30,000; 15,000; 20,000; 22,500

G = 30,000; 15,000; 7,500; 20,000; 22,500; 10,000; 11,250

Task 1.6

When a company has a period of account that exceeds 12 months, how are the following apportioned?

	Time apportioned	Separate computation	Period in which arises
Trading income	✓		
Capital allowances		✓	
Rental income	✓		
Interest income			✓
Chargeable gains			✓

Task 1.7

A company has the following non-current (fixed) asset information for the year ended 30 November 2011:

Balances brought forward as at 1 December 2010:

	£
Main pool	265,400
Managing Director's car (purchased pre April 2009)	
(BMW) – 70% private usage	18,705
Finance Director's car (purchased pre April 2009)	13,600
Additions:	
Machinery (1 June 2011)	88,897
Energy saving plant (10 August 2011)	13,900
Office furniture (1 October 2011)	22,405
Managing Director's car (Ford) (1 May 2011)	
CO_2 emissions 170g/km	32,100
Disposals:	
Machinery	11,250
Managing Director's car (BMW)	15,400

Calculate the total capital allowances and show the balances to carry forward to the next accounting period.

....

Section 2

Task 2.1

For each statement, tick the appropriate box.

	Chargeable Asset	Exempt Asset
(1) Vintage car	☐	☑
(2) Antique vase	☑	☐
(3) Racehorse	☐	☑

....

Task 2.2

Travellers Ltd sold a valuable picture for £12,000 in November 2011. This was bought for £4,000 in August 2003. The indexation factor from August 2003 to November 2011 was 0.290.

Complete the following computation:

	£
Proceeds	12,000
Cost	4,000
Indexation allowance	1160
Gain	6840
Chattel exemption	10,000

....

Task 2.3

Pressure Ltd bought 5,000 shares in Lucky Ltd for £15,500 in October 2003. A rights issue of 1 for 50 shares was bought in July 2005 for £2 per share. In December 2011, Pressure Ltd sold all the shares for £9 per share.

Indexation factors were: October 2003 to July 2005: 0.114; July 2005 to December 2011: 0.223

What is the gain made on these shares?

	NO. OF SHARES	COST	INDEXED COST
OCT 03 ACQUISITION	5000	15,500	15.500
JUL 05 INDEXED RISE			1767
JUL 05 RIGHTS 1:50	100	200	200
	5100	15700	17467
DEC 11 INDEX RISE			3895
DISPOSAL	(5100)	(15.700)	(21362)
PROCEEDS	45,900 — 15700 —5662		
	GAIN		24538

Task 2.4

Which of the following statements is correct?

(a) A capital loss made by an individual can be carried back against capital gains made in the preceding tax year

(b) A capital loss made by an individual can be carried forward to the following tax year without offsetting it against the current year gains

(c) A capital loss made by an individual is offset against gains in the following tax year but only to the extent that it reduces those gains to the amount of the annual exempt amount

(d) A capital loss made by an individual can only be carried forward for one tax year

Task 2.5

A factory was bought for £400,000 in January 2002. In October 2011, it was sold for £600,000. In the same month another factory was bought for £550,000. The amount of the gain that can be rolled over is: 600,000
400,000

£ 150,000

Available options: £400,000; £600,000; £550,000; £200,000; £150,000; £50,000

•••

Task 2.6

True or False: indexation allowance is applied to both bonus issues and rights issues of shares

•••

Task 2.7

A taxpayer has self employed income of £70,000 for 2011/12. The amount chargeable for national insurance contributions at 2% would be: £ 27.525

•••

Task 2.8

For the following, select the appropriate date:

(1)   First instalment for tax year 2011/12

31 JAN 2012

(2)   Second instalment for tax year 2011/12

3| JUL 2012

(3)   Final instalment for tax year 2011/12

31 JAN 2013

(4)   Payment date for capital gains for 2011/12

31 JAN 2013

•••

Task 2.9

A company has the following information for the year ended 31 March 2012:

(1) Taxable total profits is £625,000

(2) Dividends received, net, are £49,500 *55,000*

(3) The company has one associated company

The computation for corporation payable is:

£

625,000 @   26%   *162,500*

Less/;

3/200 (*750,000*   -   *680,000*) x $\frac{625,000}{680,000}$ *965,07*

Corporation tax payable   *161,534.93*

Date of payment   *9 MONTHS + 1 DAY*   *1/1/13*

Task 2.10

Tick the appropriate box for each of the following statements:

	True	False
(1) An individual must retain their tax records for 2011/12 until 5 April 2018		✓
(2) If an individual is eight months late in filing their tax return for 2011/12, they will receive a penalty of £200		✓
(3) Penalties for errors made by individuals in their tax return vary from 20% to 100%		✓
(4) If a company fails to keep records for the appropriate period of time, they can be fined up to £2,000		✓

Task 2.11

Using the following information, complete the tax return below:

Boxes 16 to 30 are already complete (although not showing on the return page below)

Fill out boxes 31 to 45 using the following data:

Included in the expenses listed in the tax return, the following information is relevant:

(1) Mr Zhang has taken drawings of £30,000. This is included in the salaries.

(2) Advertising and entertaining includes: £

   Gifts to customers:

   Bottles of wine costing £15 each   2,250

   Diaries carrying the business's logo, costing £10 each   400

   Staff Christmas party for 20 employees   1,485

(3) Motor expenses include expenses relating to: £

   Delivery vans   10,403

   Sales manager's car   6,915

   Zhang's car, total cost   5,700

   (30% private usage)

(4) Depreciation was £28,019.

Business expenses

Read pages SEFN 7 to SEFN 9 of the *notes* to see what expenses are allowable for tax purposes.

	Total expenses If your annual turnover was below £73,000 you may just put your total expenses in box 30		Disallowable expenses Use this column if the figures in boxes 16 to 29 include disallowable amounts
16	Cost of goods bought for resale or goods used £ · 0 0	31	£ · 0 0
17	Construction industry - *payments to subcontractors* £ · 0 0	32	£ · 0 0
18	Wages, salaries and other staff costs £ · 0 0	33	£ 3 0 0 0 0 · 0 0
19	Car, van and travel expenses £ · 0 0	34	£ 1 7 1 0 · 0 0
20	Rent, rates, power and insurance costs £ · 0 0	35	£ · 0 0
21	Repairs and renewals of property and equipment £ · 0 0	36	£ · 0 0
22	Phone, fax, stationery and other office costs £ · 0 0	37	£ · 0 0
23	Advertising and business entertainment costs £ · 0 0	38	£ 2 2 5 0 · 0 0
24	Interest on bank and other loans £ · 0 0	39	£ · 0 0
25	Bank, credit card and other financial charges £ · 0 0	40	£ · 0 0
26	Irrecoverable debts written off £ · 0 0	41	£ · 0 0
27	Accountancy, legal and other professional fees £ · 0 0	42	£ · 0 0
28	Depreciation and loss/profit on sale of assets £ · 0 0	43	£ 2 8 0 1 9 · 0 0
29	Other business expenses £ · 0 0	44	£ · 0 0
30	Total expenses in boxes 16 to 29 £ · 0 0	45	Total disallowable expenses in boxes 31 to 44 £ 6 1 9 7 9 · 0 0

SAMPLE ASSESSMENT
BUSINESS TAX

ANSWERS

Sample assessment: answers

Section 1

Task 1.1

Motor car – capital

Rent – revenue

Repairs – revenue

··

Task 1.2

		£
Net loss		(3,785)
Add		
Depreciation	28,019	
Zhang's salary	30,000	
Gifts to customers	2,250	
Subscription to golf club	220	
Motor expenses for Zhang's car	5,700	66,189
		62,404
Less		
Capital allowances		(9,878)
Adjusted trading profits		52,526

··

Task 1.3

(1) (b)

(2) (d)

(3) (b)

(4) £9,375

··

Task 1.4

True

··

Task 1.5

30 April 2011

A = 30,000

B = 20,000

C = 10,000

31 December 2011

D = 60,000

E = 30,000

F = 20,000

G = 10,000

....

Task 1.6

Trading income – time apportioned

Capital allowances – separate computation

Rental income – time apportioned

Interest income – period in which arises

Chargeable gains – period in which arises

....

Task 1.7

	AIA/FYA £	Main pool £	MD's car £	FD's car £	Allowances £
WDV B/fwd		265,400	18,705	13,600	
Disposal			(15,400)		
Balancing allowance			3,305		3,305
AIA (non-FYA) Additions:					
Machinery	88,897				
Furniture	22,405				
	111,302				
AIA	(100,000)				100,000
	11,302				
Transfer balance to pool	(11,302)	11,302			
Non-AIA Additions			Special rate pool £		
MD's new car			32,100		
Disposal		(11,250)			
		265,452			
WDA @ 20%		(53,090)			53,090
WDA @ 10%			(3,210)		3,210
WDA @ 20%				(2,720)	2,720
FYA Addition					
Plant	13,900				
FYA @ 100%	(13,900)				13,900
Total allowances	nil				176,225
Balance carried forward		212,362	28,890	10,880	

....

Task 2.1

Vintage car – exempt

Antique vase – chargeable

Racehorse – exempt

....

Task 2.2

	£
Proceeds	12,000
Cost	4,000
Indexation allowance	1,160
Gain	6,840
Chattel exemption	10,000

....

Task 2.3

	No of shares	£	£
October 2003	5,000	15,500	15,500
IA – 0.114			1,767
			17,267
RI	100	200	200
	5,100	15,700	17,467
IA – 0.223			3,895
			21,362
Disposal	(5,100)	(15,700)	(21,362)
	0	0	0
Proceeds		45,900	
Cost		(15,700)	
Indexation allowance (21,362 – 15,700)		(5,662)	
Gain		24,538	

....

Task 2.4

(c)

....

Task 2.5

£150,000

....

Task 2.6

False

....

Task 2.7

70,000 – 42,475 = *27,525*

....

Task 2.8

(1) 31 January 2012

(2) 31 July 2012

(3) 31 January 2013

(4) 31 January 2013

• •

Task 2.9

			£
625,000	@	26%	162,500.00

Less:

3/200 (750,000 − 680,000) x 625,000 / 680,000   965.07

Corporation tax payable   161,534.93

Date of payment   1-1-13

• •

Task 2.10

(1) **False**

(2) **False**

(3) **False**

(4) **False**

• •

Task 2.11

Box 33 = 30,000

Box 34 = 1,710

Box 38 = 2,250

Box 43 = 28,019

Box 45 = 61,979

• •

PRACTICE ASSESSMENT 1
BUSINESS TAX

Time allowed: 2 hours

Taxation tables

Capital allowances

Writing down allowance

Plant and machinery	20%
Annual investment allowance	£100,000

First year allowance

Energy saving and water efficient plant	100%

Motor cars

CO_2 emissions up to 110g/km (low emission cars)	100%
CO_2 emissions between 111g/km and 160g/km	20%
CO_2 emissions over 160g/km	10%

National insurance contributions

Class 2 contributions	£2.50 per week
Small earnings exception	£5,315 per year
Class 4 contributions	
Main rate	9%
Additional rate	2%
Lower profits limit	£7,225
Upper profits limit	£42,475

Corporation tax

Financial year	2011	2010
Small profits rate	20%	21%
Lower limit	300,000	300,000
Upper limit	1,500,000	1,500,000
Standard fraction	3/200	7/400
Main rate	26%	28%

Formula: Fraction × (U – A) × N/A

Capital gains tax

Rate of tax

Standard rate	18%
Higher rate (applicable over £35,000)	28%
Entrepreneurs' relief rate	10%
Annual exempt amount	£10,600

Entrepreneurs' relief

Lifetime limit	£10,000,000

Business Tax Practice Assessment 1

Section 1

Task 1.1

For the following items of expenditure, tick if they are revenue or capital:

	Revenue	Capital
Purchase of premises	☐	✓
Rent on premises	✓	☐
Heating of premises	✓	☐

Task 1.2

The income statement (profit and loss account) for George Checkers for the year ended 5 April 2012 shows:

	£	£
Gross profit		396,550
General expenses (Note 1)	85,480	
Impairment losses (bad debts) (Note 2)	585	
Motor expenses (Note 3)	7,880	
Wages and salaries	54,455	
Depreciation	21,080 ✗	
		(169,480)
Net profit		227,070

Notes

(1) General expenses include:

	£
Gifts to customers – Christmas cakes costing £4.50 each	1,350 ✗
Building a new wall around car park	2,200 ✗

(2) Impairment losses are made up of:

	£
Trade debts written-off	350
Increase in general provision	400✗
Trade debts recovered	(165)
	585

(3) Motor expenses

	Private usage	Annual expenses
	%	£
George	1650✗ 25	6,600
Salesman	20	1,280

(4) Capital allowances

Computed to be £15,000

Using the pro forma layout provided, calculate the taxable trading profit for the year ended 5 April 2012.

	£	£
NET PROFIT		227,070
ADD: GIFTS TO CUSTOMERS	1350	
NEW WALL	2200	
INCREASE GEN¹ PROVISION	400	
MOTOR EXPENSES	1650	
DEPRECIATION	21080	
		26,680
		253,750
LESS: CAPITAL ALLOWANCES		(15,000)
TAXABLE TRADING PROFIT		238,750

Task 1.3

You have received the following e-mail from Milton.

From:	milton007@boxmail.net
To:	AATStudent@boxmail.net
Sent:	27 September 2012 16:22
Subject:	Important news

You were kind enough to prepare my last set of accounts for the year to 30 June 2012 which showed a trading profit of £42,000. This was only a little down on the trading profit of £45,000 which we achieved for the year to 30 June 2011.

I have now decided that I want to sell the business and I have had a good offer for it. I will therefore cease to trade on 30 November 2012.

I was wondering how the business income will be assessed in the closing years. I hope to make a profit in the five months from 1 July 2012 to 30 November 2012 of about £15,000.

Thank you for your advice.

Milton

Reply to Milton's e-mail, explaining which profit periods will be assessed for the last two tax years. You should also mention how any overlap profits will be relieved.

Note. Assume all tax rules are the same in 2012/13 as for 2011/12.

From:	AATStudent@boxmail.net
To:	milton007@boxmail.net
Sent:	1 October 2012
Subject:	Re: Important news

Task 1.4

True or False: a sole trader must make a claim to set a loss made in 2011/12 against total income in 2011/12 before making a claim to set the loss against total income in 2010/11.

Task 1.5

Jude and Kelly have been in partnership for many years making up accounts to 30 September each year. They share profits 3:1 respectively.

On 1 July 2011, Liam joined the partnership. It was agreed that Liam would be paid a salary of £6,000 per year and that profits would be shared 2:2:1 for Jude, Kelly and Liam.

For the year ended 30 September 2011, the partnership trading profit was £54,000.

Using the pro forma layout provided, show the division of profit between the partners for the year ended 30 September 2011.

	Total	Jude	Kelly	Liam
	£	£	£	£
Period to:				
30 Jun 2011	40,500	30,375	10,125	—
Period to:				
30 Sep 2011	1500	—	—	1500
	12000	4800	4800	2400
Total profit for y/e 30.9.11	54,000	35175	14925	3900

Task 1.6

A company made up accounts to 31 December 2010. It decides to make up its next set of accounts to 31 March 2012.

How will the company deal with its capital allowances in the long period of account?

A One computation from 1 January 2011 to 31 March 2012

B Two computations: one from 1 January 2011 to 31 March 2011 and one from 1 April 2011 to 31 March 2012

C Two computations: one from 1 January 2011 to 31 December 2011 and one from 1 January 2012 to 31 March 2012

D It can deal with the computation for whatever period the company chooses

Practice assessment 1: questions

Task 1.7

You have been asked to compute the capital allowances for Mr Wish who makes up accounts to 5 April each year using the following information:

(1) The balance of the main pool at 6 April 2011 was £18,440.

(2) New machinery was bought in August 2011 for £105,400.

(3) A car with CO_2 emissions of 100g/km was bought in September 2011 for £12,000 for a salesman.

(4) A car with CO_2 emissions of 140g/km was bought in December 2011 for £16,000. Mr Wish used this car 75% of the time for business purposes.

Using the pro forma layout provided, calculate the capital allowances for Mr Wish for the year ended 5 April 2012 and show the balances to carry forward to the next accounting period.

	AIA £	FYA £	MAIN POOL £	75% CAR £	ALLOWANCES £
YE 5 APR 2012					
BALANCE B/F			18,440		
AIA ADDITIONS					
AUG - MACHINERY	105400				
AIA	(100,000)				100,000
	5,400				
TRANSFER TO MAIN POOL	(5,400)		5400		
FYA 100% CAR		12,000			
FYA 100%		(12,000)			12,000
DEC 11 CAR			23,840	16,000	
WDA 20%			(4768)	(3,200)	7168
BALANCES C/F			19072	12,800	
MAX. CAPITAL ALLOWANCE					119168

126

Section 2

Task 2.1

For the following assets, tick if a disposal would be exempt or chargeable:

	Exempt	Chargeable
Vintage car worth £40,000	✓	☐
Van worth £6,000	☐	✓
Holiday cottage worth £80,000	☐	✓

Task 2.2

Nick bought a five-acre plot of land for £50,000. He sold three acres of the land at auction for £105,000 in August 2011. He had spent £2,500 installing drainage on the three acres which he sold. His disposal costs were £1,500. The market value of the remaining two acres at the date of sale was £45,000.

The gain on sale of the three acres is:

A   £66,000

B   £66,750

C   £71,000

D   £67,500

$$\frac{105,000}{105,000 + 45,000} \times 50,000 = 35,000$$

105,000
(1500)
(35,000)
(2500)

Task 2.3

In May 2011, Green Ltd sold 4,000 of the shares it held in Blue Ltd for £130,000. These shares had been acquired as follows:

	No of shares	£
April 1987	2,000	25,000
June 1992	2,000	35,000
July 1995 – bonus issue	1 for 10	
September 2000 – rights issue	1 for 5	£10 per share

Indexation factors

April 1987 to June 1992	0.373
June 1992 to July 1995	0.074
June 1992 to September 2000	0.239
July 1995 to September 2000	0.154
September 2000 to May 2011	0.345

Using the pro forma layout provided, show the share pool and the gain on sale in May 2011.

FA 1985 pool

	No. of shares	Cost	Indexed cost
		£	£
APR 1987 ACQUISITION	2000	25,000	25,000
JUN 92 INDEXED RISE			9325
JUN 92 ACQUISITION	2000	35,000	35000
	4000	60,000	69325
JUL 95 BONUS ISSUE	400	–	–
SEP 2000 INDEX RISE			16569
SEP 2000 RIGHTS ISSUE	880	8800	8800
	5280	68800	94694
MAY 2011 INDEX RISE			32669
	5280	68800	127363
MAY 2011 DISPOSAL	(4000)	(52 121)	(96487)
BALANCE c/f	1280	16679	30876

Gain

	£
PROCEEDS	130,000
LESS : COST	(52121)
LESS : INDEXATION (96487-52121)	(44366)
GAIN ON DISPOSAL	33513

Task 2.4

True or False: if an individual has allowable losses brought forward, these are only used to bring gains down to the annual exempt amount.

Task 2.5

In November 2011, Cowley Ltd sold its factory for £260,000. It bought the factory in December 2003 for £150,000. In March 2011, it bought a replacement factory for £230,000 and claimed rollover relief. The indexation factor between December 2003 to November 2011 is 0.275

(1) The gain on the disposal is:

£ 68750

260,000
(150,000)
(41,250)
_____
68750

(2) The gain immediately chargeable is:

£ 30,000

(3) The gain rolled-over:

£ 38,750

Task 2.6

True or False: indexation allowance can increase a loss made by a company.

Task 2.7

Crystal is a sole trader who has taxable trading profits of £91,751 for the year ended 31 December 2011.

The total National Insurance Contributions payable by Crystal for the tax year 2011/12 are:

A   £4,158.02

B   £4,288.02

C   £3,302.50

D   £7,607.34

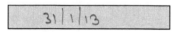

$52 \times 2.50 \qquad = 130.00$

$(42,475 - 7225) = 3172.50$

$91,751 - 42425 \qquad \underline{\quad 985.52 \quad}$

4288.02

Task 2.8

Mina has income tax payable for 2011/12 of £4,225. She was not required to make any payments on account.

(1) State the date by which the tax payable should be paid:

31/1/13

(2) Calculate the amount of each payment on account for 2012/13

£   2112   .   50

(3) State the dates by which the payments on account for 2012/13 should be paid:

31/1/13

and

31/7/13

Task 2.9

Abbey Ltd has the following information for the year ended 31 March 2012.

The adjusted trading profit, after deducting capital allowances, was £620,843.

The company sold a piece of investment land in December 2011 realising a gain of £67,817.

Abbey Ltd has one wholly owned subsidiary.

(1) Abbey Ltd's taxable total profits are:

£   688660

688660 @ 26% = 179,051·60
                = (920 ·10)

(2) The applicable upper limit is:

£   750,000

and the applicable lower limit is:

3/200 x (750.000 - 688660)

£   150,000

(3) The corporation tax payable for the year ended 31 March 2012 is:

£   178131   .   50

(4) The due date for payment is:

1 | 1 | 13

....

Task 2.10

T Ltd, a large company, has a corporation tax liability of £600,000 in respect of its accounting year end 31 December 2011.

On which date will the company be required to pay its FINAL instalment of the liability?

A   14 October 2011

B   14 January 2012

Ⓒ   14 April 2012

D   1 October 2012

....

Task 2.11

Complete the following extract from the tax return for Spire Ltd for the year ended 31 March 2012 using the information below.

The adjusted trading profit, after deducting capital allowances was £564,960.

The company sold a piece of investment land in August 2011 realising a gain of £73,240.

Spire Ltd has one wholly owned subsidiary.

Corporation tax liability was (£165,932.00 less marginal relief of £1,677.00) £164,255.00.

Page 2

Company tax calculation

Turnover

1	Total turnover from trade or profession	**1** £	

Income

3	Trading and professional profits	**3** £ 564,960	
4	Trading losses brought forward claimed against profits	**4** £	
5	Net trading and professional profits	box 3 minus box 4 **5** £ 564,960	
6	Bank, building society or other interest, and profits and gains from non-trading loan relationships	**6** £	
11	Income from UK land and buildings	**11** £	
14	Annual profits and gains not falling under any other heading	**14** £	

Chargeable gains

16	Gross chargeable gains	**16** £ 73.240
17	Allowable losses including losses brought forward	**17** £
18	Net chargeable gains	box 16 minus box 17 **18** £ 73240

21 Profits before other deductions and reliefs — sum of boxes 5, 6, 11, 11 & 18 **21** £ 638.200

Deductions and Reliefs

24	Management expenses under S75 ICTA 1988	**24** £
30	Trading losses of this or a later accounting period under S393A ICTA 1988	**30** £
31	Put an 'X' in box 31 if amounts carried back from later accounting periods are included in box 30	**31**
32	Non-trade capital allowances	**32** £
35	Charges paid	**35** £

37 Taxable total profits — box 21 minus boxes 24, 30, 32 and 35 **37** £ 638 200

Tax calculation

38	Franked investment income	**38** £ 0
39	Number of associated companies in this period or	**39** 1
40	Associated companies in the first financial year	**40**
41	Associated companies in the second financial year	**41**
42	Put an 'X' in box 42 if the company claims to be charged at the starting rate or the small companies' rate on any part of its profits, or is claiming marginal rate relief	**42** ☒

Enter how much profit has to be charged and at what rate of tax

Financial year (yyyy)	Amount of profit	Rate of tax	Tax
43 2011	**44** £ 638,200	**45** 26%	**46** £ 165,932 . 00 p
53	**54** £	**55**	**56** £ p

total of boxes 46 and 56 **63** £ 165,932 00 p

63	Corporation tax	**63** £ 165,932 00 p
64	Marginal rate relief	**64** £ 1677. 00 p
65	Corporation tax net of marginal rate relief	**65** £ 164 255 . 00 p
66	Underlying rate of corporation tax	**66** . %
67	Profits matched with non-corporate distributions	**67**
68	Tax at non-corporate distributions rate	**68** £ p
69	Tax at underlying rate on remaining profits	**69** £ p
70	Corporation tax chargeable	See note for box 70 in CT600 Guide **70** £ 164,255 00 p

CT600 (Short) (2008) Version 2

PRACTICE ASSESSMENT 1
BUSINESS TAX

ANSWERS

Business Tax Practice Assessment 1 – Answers

Section 1

Task 1.1

	Revenue	Capital
Purchase of premises		✓
Rent on premises	✓	
Heating of premises	✓	

Task 1.2

	£	£
Net profit per accounts		227,070
Add: gifts to customers	1,350	
new wall (capital)	2,200	
increase in general impairment provision	400	
private motor expenses of owner (25% × £6,600)	1,650	
depreciation	21,080	
		26,680
		253,750
Less: capital allowances		(15,000)
Taxable trading profit		238,750

Tutor's note. Gifts of food are never allowable.

Task 1.3

Taxable trading profits of the year to 30 June 2011 of £45,000 are taxed in 2011/12 which is the penultimate tax year of trading.

Taxable trading profits of the year to 30 June 2012 of £42,000 plus the profits of the five months to 30 November 2012 of £15,000, giving a total of £57,000, will be taxed in 2012/13 which is the final tax year of trading.

Any overlap profits will be relieved by deducting them from these profits in 2012/13.

Task 1.4

False

A sole trader can make a claim to deduct the loss from total income in the tax year preceding the tax year in which the loss is made whether or not he makes a claim to set it against total income in the tax year of the loss.

Note that this rule is different from that applicable to companies where a current period claim must be made before a carry-back claim.

•••

Task 1.5

	Total	Jude	Kelly	Liam
	£	£	£	£
Period to: 30 June 2011				
Profits 3:1	40,500	30,375	10,125	0
Period to: 30 September 2011				
Salary (3 months)	1,500	0	0	1,500
	12,000	4,800	4,800	2,400
Total profit for y/e 30.9.11	54,000	35,175	14,925	3,900

•••

Task 1.6

C

Two computations: one from 1 January 2011 to 31 December 2011 and one from 1 January 2012 to 31 March 2012.

•••

Task 1.7

	AIA £	100% FYA £	Main pool £	Owner's car £	Allowances £
b/f			18,440		
AIA only additions					
Plant	105,400				
AIA	(100,000)				100,000
	5,400				
Transfer to main pool	(5,400)		5,400		
			23,840		
Non-AIA additions					
Car		12,000			
100% FYA		(12,000)			12,000
Car				16,000	
WDA @ 20%			(4,768)	(3,200) × 75%	7,168
c/f			19,072	12,800	
Capital allowances					119,168

....

Section 2

Task 2.1

	Exempt	Chargeable
Vintage car worth £40,000	✓	
Van worth £6,000		✓
Holiday cottage worth £80,000		✓

Task 2.2

A

	£
Proceeds of sale	105,000
Less: costs of disposal	(1,500)
Net proceeds	103,500
Less: cost	

$$\frac{105,000}{105,000 + 45,000} \times £50,000 \qquad (35,000)$$

	£
enhancement expenditure	(2,500)
Chargeable gain	66,000

Task 2.3

FA 1985 pool

	No of shares	Cost £	Indexed cost £
April 1987	2,000	25,000	25,000
Index to June 1992 0.373 × £25,000			9,325
	2,000	25,000	34,325
Addition	2,000	35,000	35,000
	4,000	60,000	69,325
Bonus issue (N)	400	–	–
	4,400	60,000	69,325
Index to September 2000 0.239 × £69,325			16,569
	4,400	60,000	85,894
Rights issue	880	8,800	8,800
	5,280	68,800	94,694
Index to May 2011 0.345 × £94,694			32,669
	5,280	68,800	127,363
Less: sale	(4,000)	(52,121)	(96,487)
	1,280	16,679	30,876

Gain

	£
Disposal proceeds	130,000
Less: cost	(52,121)
indexation (£96,487 – £52,121)	(44,366)
Chargeable gain	33,513

Note. There is no need to compute indexation to the date of the bonus issue.

Task 2.4

True

If an individual has allowable losses brought forward, these are only used to bring gains down to the annual exempt amount. (Compare with current year losses which are used as far as possible before deduction of the annual exempt amount.)

Task 2.5

(1)

		£
Sale proceeds		260,000
Less: cost		(150,000)
indexation allowance £150,000 × 0.275		(41,250)
Chargeable gain		**68,750**

(2) **£30,000** of the gain is immediately chargeable, as this amount of the proceeds is not reinvested in the replacement factory.

(3) **£38,750** of the gain is rolled-over. This amount of the gain is set against the base cost of the replacement factory.

•••

Task 2.6

False

Indexation allowance can only reduce a gain to nil, it cannot create or increase a loss.

•••

Task 2.7

B

		£
Class 2	£2.50 × 52	130.00
Class 4	£(42,475 – 7,225) × 9%	3,172.50
	£(91,751 – 42,475) × 2%	985.52
		4,288.02

•••

Task 2.8

(1) The balance is payable by **31 January 2013**.

(2) Payments on account for 2012/13 are £4,225 ÷ 2 = **£2,112.50**.

(3) Payments on account for 2012/13 should be paid by **31 January 2013** and **31 July 2013**.

•••

Task 2.9

(1)

	£
Adjusted trading profit	620,843
Chargeable gain	67,817
Taxable total profits	688,660

(2) There is one associated company, so the small profits lower and upper limits must be divided by 2:

Upper limit = **£750,000**

Lower limit = **£150,000**

(3) Marginal relief applies:

	£
£688,660 × 26%	179,051.60
Less: 3/200 × (£750,000 – £688,660)	(920.10)
	178,131.50

(4) £178,131.50 must be paid by **1 January 2013**

••

Task 2.10

C

The final instalment is due on 14 April 2012.

••

Task 2.11

Box 3	£564,960
Box 5	£564,960
Box 16	£73,240
Box 18	£73,240
Box 21	£638,200
Box 37	£638,200
Box 39	1
Box 42	X
Box 43	2011
Box 44	£638,200
Box 45	26%
Box 46	£165,932.00
Box 63	£165,932.00
Box 64	£1,677.00
Box 65	£164,255.00
Box 70	£164,255.00

PRACTICE ASSESSMENT 2
BUSINESS TAX

Time allowed: 2 hours

Taxation tables

Capital allowances

Writing down allowance

Plant and machinery	20%
Annual investment allowance	£100,000

First year allowance

Energy saving and water efficient plant	100%

Motor cars

CO_2 emissions up to 110g/km (low emission cars)	100%
CO_2 emissions between 111g/km and 160g/km	20%
CO_2 emissions over 160g/km	10%

National insurance contributions

Class 2 contributions	£2.50 per week
Small earnings exception	£5,315 per year
Class 4 contributions	
Main rate	9%
Additional rate	2%
Lower profits limit	£7,225
Upper profits limit	£42,475

Corporation tax

Financial year	2011	2010
Small profits rate	20%	21%
Lower limit	300,000	300,000
Upper limit	1,500,000	1,500,000
Standard fraction	3/200	7/400
Main rate	26%	28%

Formula: Fraction × (U – A) × N/A

Capital gains tax

Rate of tax

Standard rate	18%
Higher rate (applicable over £35,000)	28%
Entrepreneurs' relief rate	10%
Annual exempt amount	£10,600

Entrepreneurs' relief

Lifetime limit	£10,000,000

Business Tax Practice Assessment 2

Section 1

Task 1.1

For the following items of expenditure, tick if they are revenue or capital:

	Revenue	Capital
Purchase of raw materials	✓	☐
Purchase of delivery van	☐	✓
Repainting exterior of premises	✓	☐

. . . .

Task 1.2

The income statement (profit and loss account) of Henry Ltd for the year to 31 December 2011 shows the following information:

	£	£
Gross profit		487,500
Profit on sale of shares		12,850 ✗
Dividends received		4,500 ✗
Property business income		7,500 ✗
		512,350
General expenses (Note 1)	240,780	
Wages and salaries	120,650	
Administrative expenses	87,230	
Depreciation	14,600 ✓	
		(463,260)
Net profit		49,090

Notes

(1) **General expenses**

These include:

	£
Gift Aid donation (paid July 2011)	3,500 ✗
Entertaining customers	8,450 ✗

(2) **Capital allowances**

The capital allowances for the year ended 31 December 2011 are £8,750

Using the pro forma layout provided, compute the adjusted trading profit for Henry Ltd for the year to 31 December 2011.

	£	£
NET PROFIT		49,090
ADD: GIFT AID	3500	
ENTERTAIN CUSTOMERS	8450	
DEPRECIATION	14600	26,550
		75640
LESS: PROFIT ON SALE	12850	
DIV. REC	4500	
PROP. BUSINESS INCOME	7500	
CAPITAL ALLOWANCES	8750	
		(33,600)
ADJUSTED TRADING PROFIT		42040

Task 1.3

Sayed started trading on 1 January 2011. He makes up his accounts to 30 April each year. The profits were calculated as:

	£
Period to 30 April 2011	20,000
Year to 30 April 2012	36,000
Year to 30 April 2013	42,000

(handwritten: 56,000)

(handwritten annotations:)
2010/41   1/1/11 – 5/4/11
2011/12   1/1/11 – 30/12/11
2012/13   1/5/11 – 30/4/12

(1) The tax year in which he started trading was:

A   2009/10   *2010/11 1/1/11 – 5/4/11*

B   2010/11

C   2011/12   *2011/12 1/1/11 – 31/12/11*

D   2012/13   *2012/13 1/5/11   30/4/12*

(2) His taxable profits in his first tax year of trading were:

A   £14,000

B   £15,000   *(handwritten: $\frac{20000}{4} \times 3 = £15,000$)*

C   £20,000

D   £24,000

(handwritten right:)
15,000
44,000
36,000
95,000

(3) His taxable profits in his second tax year of trading were:

A   £20,000

B   £36,000   *20,000*

C   £42,000   *$\frac{36,000}{12} \times 8$ 24,000*

D   £44,000   *44,000*

(handwritten right:)
95,000
(56,000)
39,000

(4) His taxable profits in his third tax year of trading were:

A   £24,000

B   £36,000   *36,000*

C   £39,000

D   £42,000

(5) His overlap profits are:

£ | 39,000 |

....

Task 1.4

True or False: a company can set-off its allowable losses on the disposal of chargeable assets against trading profits.

....

Task 1.5

Gerry and Harold have been in partnership for many years making up accounts to 31 December each year sharing profits 2:1 respectively.

On 1 January 2012, Iris joined the partnership. Profits are then shared 2:2:1 for Gerry, Harold and Iris.

For the year ended 31 December 2011, the partnership trading profit was £27,000 and for the year ended 31 December 2012 was £35,000

(1) Using the pro forma layout provided, show the division of profit between the partners for the year ended 31 December 2011 and 31 December 2012.

	Total	Gerry	Harold	Iris
	£	£	£	£
Year ended 31.12.11	27,000	18,000	9000	—
Year ended 31.12.12	35,000	14,000	14000	7000

(2) The taxable trading profit for each partner for 2011/12 is:

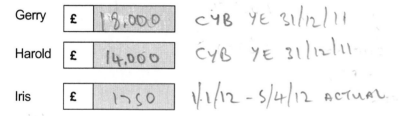

Gerry £ 18,000 CYB YE 31/12/11

Harold £ 14,000 CYB YE 31/12/11

Iris £ 1750 1/1/12 – 5/4/12 ACTUAL

. . . .

Task 1.6

A company made up accounts to 31 March 2011. It decides to make up its next set of accounts to 30 September 2012.

True or false: the company will compute trading income separately for each accounting period within the long period of account

WILL APPORTION PROFITS ON TIME BASIS
BETWEEN THE A/C PERIODS

Task 1.7

Angela ceased trading on 5 January 2012 when she sold her business as a going concern to Sarah Watson. Angela had made up accounts to 5 April each year.

On 6 April 2011, the balances for capital allowances purposes were:

	£
Main pool	7,330
Car, private usage 30%	9,570

The plant and machinery in the main pool was sold to Sarah Watson on 5 January 2012 for £8,200. Angela decided to keep the car after the business ceased trading. The market value of the car on 5 January 2012 was £6,000. It had originally cost £15,570.

Using the pro forma layout provided, compute the capital allowances to the date of cessation.

	MAIN POOL	30% PRIVATE CAR	ALLOWANCES
	£	£	£
6/4/11 BALANCE B/F	7330	9570	
5/1/12 DISPOSAL PLANT & M/c	(8200)		
BALANCING CHARGE	(870)		(870)
5/1/12 MARKET VALUE CAR		(6000)	
		3570	2499
CAPITAL ALLOWANCES			1629

Section 2

Task 2.1

For the following assets, tick if a disposal would be exempt or chargeable:

	Exempt	Chargeable
Greyhound worth £10,000	✓	☐
Lorry worth £12,000	☐	✓
Shares in quoted company worth £5,000	☐	✓

Task 2.2

Old Ltd bought a plot of land in November 2007 for £70,000. It paid legal fees of £1,500 on the acquisition. Old Ltd sold the land for £125,000 in March 2012. It spent £500 advertising the land and £1,800 on legal fees.

Indexation factor

November 2007 to March 2012   0.154

The chargeable gain on the sale is:

£ 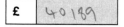 40,189

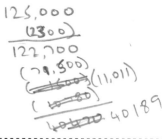

```
125,000
 (2300)
122,700
 (79,800) (11,011)
 (       )
          40,189
```

Task 2.3

Purple Ltd had the following transactions in the shares of Yellow Ltd:

May 1987	Purchased 4,000 shares for £8,000
May 2001	Took up one for two rights issue at £3 per share
October 2011	Sold all the shares for £32,000

Indexation factors

May 1987 to May 2001	0.745
May 2001 to October 2011	0.330

Using the pro forma layout provided, calculate the chargeable gain arising from the sale of the shares in Yellow Ltd.

Share pool

	No of shares	Cost	Indexed cost
		£	£
MAY 87 PURCHASE	4000	8000	8000
MAY 01 INDEX RISE			5960
	4000	8000	13960
MAY 01 RIGHTS ISSUE 1:2	2000	6000	6000
	6000	14000	19960
OCT 11 INDEX RISE			6587
	6000	14000	26547
OCT 11 DISPOSAL	(6000)	(14000)	(26547)
C/F	0	0	0

Gain

	£
PROCEEDS	32,000
LESS : COST	(14,000)
LESS : INDEXED COST (26547 - 14000)	(12547)
GAIN ON SALE	5453

Task 2.4

Georgia sold her business which she had run for twenty years to Milly on 10 October 2011. The only chargeable asset was her shop which Georgia had bought in February 2005 for £82,500. She spent £17,000 on building an extension in June 2007. The sale proceeds relating to the shop were £225,000. Georgia claimed entrepreneurs' relief on the disposal.

Using the pro forma layout provided, calculated Georgia's capital gains tax liability for 2011/12. She had made no other chargeable gains during the year.

	£
SALE PROCEEDS	225,000
LESS: COST	(82,500)
LESS ENHANCEMENT	(17,000)
	125,500
LESS: ANNUAL EXEMPT AMOUNT	(10,600)
	114,900
CG TAX PAYABLE @ 10%	11,490.00

Task 2.5

On 1 November 2011 Mike sold a factory used in his business for £600,000. The factory had cost £175,000. Mike had purchased a replacement factory for £750,000 on 1 September 2011.

How much of Mike's capital gain on the disposal of the original factory can be deferred by a rollover relief claim?

A £150,000

B £575,000   600,000

C £175,000   (175,000)

D £425,000   425,000

Task 2.6

True or False: a company is entitled to an annual exempt amount to set against chargeable gains.

Task 2.7

Polly is a sole trader who has taxable trading profits of £63,000.

The amount chargeable to national insurance Class 4 contributions at 2% is:

£   2052 5

Task 2.8

Holly has a liability to capital gains tax in 2011/12.

She must pay the capital gains tax due by:

31/1/13

Task 2.9

Merry plc had the following results for a nine-month accounting period to 31 March 2012:

		£
Taxable total profits	1,125,000	1,000,000
Dividends received	225,000	180,000 $\times \frac{100}{90}$

1,1....

Merry plc's corporation tax liability for the year is:

£   260,000 .   00

Task 2.10

Tick the appropriate box for each of the following statements:

	True	False
If a company makes a careless error in its tax return, the maximum penalty payable is 70%		✓
Capital gains tax for 2011/12 is payable on 31 January 2013	✓	
An individual who is a sole trader must retain all tax records for 2011/12 until 31 January 2018	✓	

Task 2.11

Aggie Tring has carried on business for many years as a furniture restorer making up accounts to 31 December each year.

The following information is relevant to her period of account to 31 December 2011:

	£
Revenue (turnover)	144,000
Cost of materials used in restoration	20,000
Travel (20% private)	5,700
Electricity	900
Insurance	360
Office costs	1,800
Bank charges	200
Accountancy	550
Machinery purchased	5,000

Using this information, complete the self employment page.

Business expenses

Read pages SEFN 7 to SEFN 9 of the *notes* to see what expenses are allowable for tax purposes.

Total expenses	Disallowable expenses
If your annual turnover was below £73,000 you may just put your total expenses in box 30	Use this column if the figures in boxes 16 to 29 include disallowable amounts

16 Cost of goods bought for resale or goods used
£ 20000 · 0 0

31
£ · 0 0

17 Construction industry - *payments to subcontractors*
£ · 0 0

32
£ · 0 0

18 Wages, salaries and other staff costs
£ · 0 0

33
£ · 0 0

19 Car, van and travel expenses
£ 5700 · 0 0

34
£ 1140 · 0 0

20 Rent, rates, power and insurance costs
£ 1260 · 0 0

35
£ · 0 0

21 Repairs and renewals of property and equipment
£ · 0 0

36
£ · 0 0

22 Phone, fax, stationery and other office costs
£ 1800 · 0 0

37
£ · 0 0

23 Advertising and business entertainment costs
£ · 0 0

38
£ · 0 0

24 Interest on bank and other loans
£ · 0 0

39
£ · 0 0

25 Bank, credit card and other financial charges
£ 200 · 0 0

40
£ · 0 0

26 Irrecoverable debts written off
£ · 0 0

41
£ · 0 0

27 Accountancy, legal and other professional fees
£ 550 · 0 0

42
£ · 0 0

28 Depreciation and loss/profit on sale of assets
£ · 0 0

43
£ · 0 0

29 Other business expenses
£ · 0 0

44
£ · 0 0

30 Total expenses in boxes 16 to 29
£ 29510 · 0 0

45 Total disallowable expenses in boxes 31 to 44
£ 1140 · 0 0

PRACTICE ASSESSMENT 2
BUSINESS TAX

ANSWERS

Business Tax Practice Assessment 2 – Answers

Section 1

Task 1.1

	Revenue	Capital
Purchase of raw materials	✓	
Purchase of delivery van		✓
Repainting exterior of premises	✓	

•••

Task 1.2

Henry Ltd adjusted trading profit for the year ending 31 December 2011

	£	£
Net profit		49,090
Add: Gift Aid donation	3,500	
entertaining customers	8,450	
depreciation	14,600	
		26,550
		75,640
Less: profit on sale of shares	12,850	
dividends received	4,500	
property business income	7,500	
capital allowances	8,750	
		(33,600)
Adjusted trading profit		42,040

•••

Task 1.3

(1) **B**

2010/11

(2) **B**

2010/11

First tax year: actual

Basis period: 1 January 2011 to 5 April 2011

Taxable trading profits ¾ × £20,000 = £15,000

(3) **D**

2011/12

Second tax year: first 12 months of trading

Basis period: 1 January 2011 to 31 December 2011

Taxable trading profits £20,000 + 8/12 × £36,000 = £44,000

(4) **B**

2012/13

Third tax year: 12 months to accounting date ending in tax year

Basis period: 1 May 2011 to 30 April 2012

Taxable trading profits £36,000

(5) Overlap period: 1 January 2011 to 5 April 2011 and 1 May 2011 to 31 December 2011

Overlap profits: ¾ × £20,000 + 8/12 × £36,000 = **£39,000**

Task 1.4

False

A company can set-off its allowable losses on the disposal of chargeable assets only against chargeable gains.

Task 1.5

(1)

	Total	Gerry	Harold	Iris
	£	£	£	£
Year ended 31.12.11	27,000	18,000	9,000	0
Year ended 31.12.12	35,000	14,000	14,000	7,000

(2) *Gerry*

y/e 31.12.11 current year basis

£18,000

Harold

y/e 31.12.11 current year basis

£9,000

Iris

First year of trading: actual basis 1 January 2012 to 5 April 2012

3/12 × £7,000 = **£1,750**

Task 1.6

False

The company will apportion its trading profits for the long period of account on a time basis between the accounting periods.

Task 1.7

Capital allowances to the date of cessation

	Main pool	Private use car	Allowances
	£	£	£
B/f	7,330	9,570	
Proceeds	(8,200)	(6,000)	
	(870)	3,570	
Balancing charge	870		(870)
Balancing allowance		(3,570) × 70%	2,499
Allowances			1,629

Section 2

Task 2.1

For the following assets, tick if a disposal would be exempt or chargeable:

	Exempt	Chargeable
Greyhound worth £10,000	✓	
Lorry worth £12,000		✓
Shares in quoted company worth £5,000		✓

Task 2.2

	£
Proceeds of sale	125,000
Less: costs of disposal £(500 + 1,800)	(2,300)
Net proceeds	122,700
Less: cost £(70,000 + 1,500)	(71,500)
	51,200
Less: indexation allowance 0.154 × £71,500	(11,011)
Chargeable gain	**40,189**

Task 2.3

Share pool

	No of shares	Cost £	Indexed cost £
May 1987	4,000	8,000	8,000
Indexed rise to May 2001			
£8,000 × 0.745			5,960
			13,960
Rights issue 1:2 @ £3	2,000	6,000	6,000
	6,000	14,000	19,960
Indexed rise to October 2011			
£19,960 × 0.330			6,587
	6,000	14,000	26,547

Gain

	£
Disposal proceeds	32,000
Less: cost	(14,000)
	18,000
Less: indexation (£26,547 – £14,000)	(12,547)
Chargeable gain	5,453

....

Task 2.4

	£
Sale proceeds	225,000
Less: cost	(82,500)
enhancement expenditure	(17,000)
	125,500
Less: annual exempt amount	(10,600)
Taxable gains	114,900
CGT payable £114,900 @ 10%	11,490.00

....

Task 2.5

D

	£
Proceeds	600,000
Less: cost	(175,000)
Chargeable gain	425,000

Mike reinvested all of the proceeds in a replacement business asset in the period 12 months before/3 years after the disposal so the whole gain of £425,000 can be rolled-over.

....

Task 2.6

False

Only an individual is entitled to an annual exempt amount to set against chargeable gains.

....

Task 2.7

£(63,000 – 42,475) = **£20,525**

Task 2.8

31 January 2013

Task 2.9

	£
Taxable total profits	1,000,000
Dividends received × 100/90	200,000
Augmented profits	1,200,000
Upper limit: £1,500,000 × 9/12	1,125,000

Main rate applies

£1,000,000 × 26%   **260,000.00**

Task 2.10

	True	False
If a company makes a careless error in its tax return, the maximum penalty payable is 70%		✓ (maximum penalty is 30%)
Capital gains tax for 2011/12 is payable on 31 January 2013	✓	
An individual who is a sole trader must retain all tax records for 2011/12 until 31 January 2018	✓	

Task 2.11

Box 16	£20000.00
Box 19	£5700.00
Box 20	£1260.00
Box 22	£1800.00
Box 25	£200.00
Box 27	£550.00
Box 30	£29510.00
Box 34	£1140.00
Box 45	£1140.00

PRACTICE ASSESSMENT 3
BUSINESS TAX

Time allowed: 2 hours

Taxation tables

Capital allowances

Writing down allowance

Plant and machinery	20%
Annual investment allowance	£100,000

First year allowance

Energy saving and water efficient plant	100%

Motor cars

CO_2 emissions up to 110g/km (low emission cars)	100%
CO_2 emissions between 111g/km and 160g/km	20%
CO_2 emissions over 160g/km	10%

National insurance contributions

Class 2 contributions	£2.50 per week
Small earnings exception	£5,315 per year
Class 4 contributions	
Main rate	9%
Additional rate	2%
Lower profits limit	£7,225
Upper profits limit	£42,475

Corporation tax

Financial year	2011	2010
Small profits rate	20%	21%
Lower limit	300,000	300,000
Upper limit	1,500,000	1,500,000
Standard fraction	3/200	7/400
Main rate	26%	28%

Formula: Fraction × (U − A) × N/A

Capital gains tax

Rate of tax

Standard rate	18%
Higher rate (applicable over £35,000)	28%
Entrepreneurs' relief rate	10%

Annual exempt amount	£10,600

Entrepreneurs' relief

Lifetime limit	£10,000,000

Business Tax Practice Assessment 3

Section 1

Task 1.1

For the following items of expenditure, tick if they are revenue or capital:

	Revenue	Capital
Repairs to existing premises	☑	☐
Insurance for premises	☑	☐
Repairs to new premises to make them usable	☐	☑

Task 1.2

You have been given the following information about Robbie Ltd that relates to the year ended 31 March 2012:

	£	£
Gross profit		801,220
Profit on sale of shares		45,777 ✗
Dividends received		40,500 ✗
		887,497
General expenses (Note 1)	455,100	
Administrative expenses	122,010	
Wages and salaries	137,567	(714,677)
Net profit		172,820

Note 1: General expenses:

These include:

	£
Gift Aid donation	5,000 ✗
Parking fines paid for a director	160 ✗
Depreciation	65,230 ✗
Subscription to a trade association	1,000
Donation to a political party	850 ✗

Note 2: Capital allowances:

These have already been calculated at £38,750.

Using the pro forma layout provided, show the adjusted trading profit for Robbie Ltd for the year to 31 March 2012.

	£	£
NET PROFIT		172.820
ADD: GIFT AID	8000	
PARKING FINE	160	
DEPRECIATION	65.230	
DONATION	850	
		71240
		244060
LESS: PROFIT ON SALE	45777	
DIVIDENDS RECEIVED	40500	
CAPITAL ALLOWANCES	38.750	(125027)
ADJUSTED TRADING PROFIT		119,033

Task 1.3

Vince started trading on 1 March 2011. He made up his first set of accounts to 30 September 2011 and thereafter to 30 September each year. The profits were calculated as:

	£
Period to 30 September 2011	14,000
Year to 30 September 2012	36,000

(1) His taxable profits in his first tax year of trading were:

A £2,000

B £3,000

C £14,000

D £24,000

Handwritten: 2010/11, 2011/12, 2012/13

Handwritten: 1/3/11 - 5/4/11
1/3/11 - 29/2/12
1/10/11 - 30/9/12

(2) His taxable profits in his second tax year of trading were:

A £14,000

B £29,000

C £30,000

D £36,000

Handwritten: 14000, 15000, 29,000

(3) His taxable profits in his third tax year of trading were:

A £24,000

B £30,000

C £36,000

D £38,000

Handwritten: 67,000, 50,000, 17,000

(4) His overlap profits are

£ *17,000*

Task 1.4

Zowie made a loss of £10,000 in her period of account to 31 March 2012.

Which ONE of the following statements is incorrect?

A Zowie can set the loss against her general income in 2011/12

B Zowie can carry the loss forward against her trading profits in 2012/13

C Zowie can set the loss against her general income in 2012/13

D Zowie can set the loss against her general income in 2010/11

Task 1.5

Melanie, Nadia and Orla have been in partnership for many years. Melanie and Nadia introduced £10,000 and £25,000 capital into the partnership. They are paid 6% interest on their investment. Orla is entitled to a salary of £9,900 a year. The remaining profits are divided 2:1:1 to Melanie, Nadia and Orla respectively.

The partnership made a profit of £48,000 in the year to 31 March 2012.

Using the pro forma layout provided, show how this profit is divided between the partners.

	Total	Melanie	Nadia	Orla
	£	£	£	£
SALARY	9900	—	—	9900
6% INTEREST	2100	600	1500	—
PROFIT SHARE	36,000	18000	9000	9000
	48000	18,600	10500	18900

Task 1.6

Z plc makes up accounts for a 15 month period to 31 March 2012.

How will the company apportion its property income for the long period of account between the accounting periods?

A   In any way the company chooses

B   On a time basis

C   On an accruals basis

D   On a receipts basis

Task 1.7

Ian Goodwin commenced trading on 1 May 2011, and made his first accounts up to 31 August 2012. Ian Goodwin's capital transactions from the date of commencement are:

Additions: £

1 May 2011	Plant and machinery	95,000
1 May 2011	Motor van	15,000
1 October 2011	Plant and machinery	30,000
1 November 2011	Car, used 30% private usage by Ian (CO₂ emissions 172g/km)	9,600

Using the pro forma layout provided, calculate the capital allowances for the 16-month period ended 31 August 2012.

	AIA	MAIN POOL	70% SPECIAL RATE POOL	ALLOWANCES
AIA ADDITIONS				
1 MAY 2011 PLANT + M/c	95,000			
1 MAY 2011 MOTOR VAN	15,000			
1 OCT 2011 PLANT + M/c	30,000			
	140,000			
LESS AIA x 16 MONTHS	(133 333)			133,333
	6667			
TRANSFER TO MAIN POOL	(6667)	6667		
NON AIA ADDITIONS				
CAR 30% PRIVATE			9600	
WDA @ 20% MAIN POOL		(1778)		1778
WDA @ 10% CAR			(1280)	896
BALANCE c/f		4889	8320	
CAPITAL ALLOWANCES				136 007

Section 2

Task 2.1

For the following assets, tick if a disposal would be exempt or chargeable:

	Exempt	Chargeable
Porsche car worth £120,000	✓	☐
Necklace sold for £5,000, cost £2,000	✓	☐
Shares in unlisted company worth £12,000	☐	✓

Task 2.2

Jakub bought a holiday cottage for £64,000 incurring legal costs of £1,200 on the purchase. He spent £12,000 on adding an extension to the cottage but had to remove it as he had not obtained planning permission.

Jakub sold the cottage for £90,000 in September 2011. He paid estate agent's fees of £1,800 and legal costs of £700.

Complete the following computation.

£

Proceeds	90,000
Disposal costs	(2500)
Costs of acquisition	(65200)
Enhancement expenditure	0
Chargeable gain	22300

Task 2.3

Treasure Ltd sold 2,500 shares in Williams Ltd for £102,100 in June 2011.

2,000 shares had been bought in November 1998 for £50,000.

In February 2003, Treasure Ltd took up a rights issue of 1 for 2 shares, at £20 per share.

Indexation factors

November 1998 to February 2003   0.118

February 2003 to June 2011   0.289

Using the pro forma layout provided, calculate the capital gain arising from the disposal of the shares in Williams Ltd. Clearly show the number of shares, and their value, to carry forward.

Share pool

		No. of shares	Cost £	Indexed cost £
NOV 98	BOUGHT	2000	50000	50,000
FEB 03	INDEX RISE			5900
		2000	50,000	55900
FEB 03	RIGHTS ISSUE	1000	20,000	20,000
		3000	70,000	75,900
JUL 11	INDEX RISE			21,935
		3000	70,000	97835
JUL 11	DISPOSAL	(2500)	(58,333)	(81,529)
	c/F	500	11667	16306

Gain

	£
PROCEEDS	102,100
COST	(58333)
INDEX	(23196)
	20571

Task 2.4

Sami gives a shop which he has used in his trade to his son Troy in August 2011. The shop was acquired for £120,000 and was worth £150,000 at the date of the gift. A claim for gift relief is made.

Which of the following statements are correct?

(A)   Troy will acquire the shop at a cost of £120,000

(B)   Sami will have no chargeable gain on the gift

C   Gift relief can be restricted to allow Sami to use his annual exempt amount

D   Troy will acquire the shop at a cost of £150,000

....

Task 2.5

DEF plc bought a factory for use in its trade on 10 December 2005 for £120,000. It sold the factory for £230,000 on 1 May 2011.

Indexation factors

December 2005 to May 2011   0.177

(1)   The gain on disposal of the factory is:

£    88760

(2)   The dates during which a new asset must be acquired for a rollover relief claim to be made are between:

 1/5/10

and

 1/5/14

(3)   If a new factory is acquired for £200,000, the amount of the gain which can be rolled-over is:

£   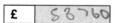 58760

....

Task 2.6

BCD Ltd acquires 1,000 shares in UVW plc on 10 June 2005. There is a rights issue on 28 November 2011 and BCD Ltd takes up its full entitlement of 200 shares. It sells 200 shares on 2 December 2011.

True or False: the 200 shares sold on 2 December 2011 will be matched with the acquisition on 28 November 2011.

....

Task 2.7

Jayden starts in business as a sole trader on 6 April 2011. Her annual profit for 2011/12 is £5,300 and her adjusted trading profit for the year to 5 April 2012 is £7,500.

(1) Jayden's Class 2 NICs payable for 2011/12 are:

£	O	.	OO

(2) Jayden's Class 4 NICs payable for 2011/12 are:

£	24	.	7S

$7500 - 7225 = 275 \times 9\%$

Task 2.8

You have been instructed by a new client who started trading on 1 May 2011. He is concerned about having missed some very important dates when he should have contacted HM Revenue & Customs. He has never filled in a tax return.

State:

(1) The date when he should have informed HM Revenue & Customs that he was liable to Class 2 contributions.

31/1/13

(2) The date when he should have informed HM Revenue & Customs that he was chargeable to income tax

5/10/12

(3) The date when his first tax return should have been filed, if it is to be filed online.

31/1/13

Task 2.9

Sweet Ltd has taxable total profits for the year ended 31 March 2012 of £139,790. It received a dividend of £40,500 from Sugar Ltd and £18,000 from Syrup Ltd. Sweet Ltd owns 60% of the shares in Syrup Ltd.

Using the pro forma layout provided, calculate the corporation tax payable by Sweet Ltd for the year ended 31 March 2012.

	£

Task 2.10

Tick the appropriate box for each of the following statements:

	True	False
A company with a period of account ending on 30 September 2011 must keep its records until 30 September 2017	☑	☐
The penalty for failing to keep records is £3,000 for each accounting period	☑	☐
A sole trader who is seven months late filing a tax return will be subject to a penalty of £200	☐	☑

Task 2.11

You act for Freshly Fish, a partnership of fishmongers. The partners are Fred Fisher and his son George. The partnership profits are divided 2:1 between Fred and George. The partnership makes up accounts to 31 March each year.

The following information relates to the year to 31 March 2012:

	£
Revenue (turnover)	210,000
Cost of fish sold	70,000
Allowable expenses	69,710
Capital allowances	13,200

Use this information to complete page 6 of the partnership tax return for Fred Fisher.

PARTNERSHIP STATEMENT (SHORT) *for the year ended 5 April 2012*

Please read these instructions before completing the Statement

Use these pages to allocate partnership income if the only income for the relevant return period was trading and professional income or taxed interest and alternative finance receipts from banks and building societies. Otherwise you must ask the SA Orderline for the *Partnership Statement (Full)* pages to record details of the allocation of all the partnership income.

 Step 1 Fill in boxes 1 to 29 and boxes A and B as appropriate. Get the figures you need from the relevant boxes in the Partnership Tax Return. Complete a separate Statement for each accounting period covered by this Partnership Tax Return and for each trade or profession carried on by the partnership.

 Step 2 Then allocate the amounts in boxes 11 to 29 attributable to each partner using the allocation columns on this page and page 7 (see pages 14 to 17 of the Partnership Tax Return Guide for help). If the partnership has more than three partners, please photocopy page 7.

 Step 3 Each partner will need a copy of their allocation of income to fill in their personal tax return.

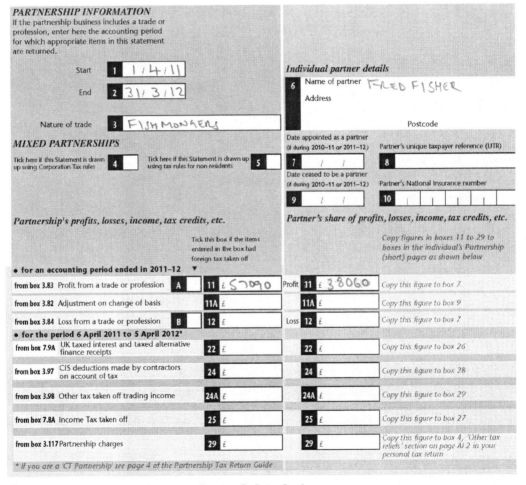

PRACTICE ASSESSMENT 3
BUSINESS TAX

ANSWERS

Business Tax Practice Assessment 3 – Answers

Section 1

Task 1.1

	Revenue	Capital
Repairs to existing premises	✓	
Insurance for premises	✓	
Repairs to new premises to make them usable		✓

....

Task 1.2

	£	£
Net profit per accounts		172,820
Add: Gift Aid donation	5,000	
director's parking fines	160	
depreciation	65,230	
donation to political party	850	71,240
		244,060
Less: profit on sale of shares	45,777	
dividends received	40,500	
capital allowances	38,750	(125,027)
Adjusted trading profit		119,033

....

Task 1.3

(1) **A**

2010/11

First tax year: actual basis

Basis period: 1 March 2011 to 5 April 2011

Taxable trading profits: $1/7 \times £14,000 = £2,000$

(2) **B**

2011/12

Second tax year: first twelve months trading

Basis period: 1 March 2011 to 28 February 2012

Taxable trading profits: $£14,000 + (5/12 \times £36,000) = £29,000$

(3) **C**

2012/13

Third tax year: period of 12 months to accounting date ending in tax year

Basis period: 1 October 2011 to 30 September 2012

Taxable trading profits: £36,000

(4) Overlap period: 1 March 2011 to 5 April 2011 and 1 October 2011 to 28 February 2012

Overlap profits: $(1/7 \times £14,000) + (5/12 \times £36,000) = $ **£17,000**

Task 1.4

C

The statement that Zowie can set the loss against her general income in 2012/13 is incorrect.

Task 1.5

	Total	Melanie	Nadia	Orla
	£	£	£	£
Interest	2,100	600	1,500	0
Salary	9,900	0	0	9,900
Profit share	36,000	18,000	9,000	9,000
Total	48,000	18,600	10,500	18,900

Task 1.6

B

On a time basis

··

Task 1.7

	AIA £	Main pool £	Car (70%) £	Allowances £
AIA additions				
Plant and machinery	95,000			
Motor van	15,000			
Plant and machinery	30,000			
	140,000			
AIA £100,000 × 16/12	(133,333)			133,333
	6,667			
Transfer balance to main pool	(6,667)	6,667		
Non-AIA addition				
Car			9,600	
WDA @ 20% × 16/12		(1,778)		1,778
WDA @ 10% × 16/12			(1,280) × 70%	896
c/f		4,889	8,320	
Allowances				136,007

Note. Both the AIA and the WDA are time apportioned for a long period of account.

··

Section 2

Task 2.1

	Exempt	Chargeable
Porsche car worth £120,000	✓	
Necklace sold for £5,000, cost £2,000	✓	
Shares in unlisted company worth £12,000		✓

Task 2.2

	£
Proceeds of sale	90,000
Disposal costs £(1,800 + 700)	(2,500)
Costs of acquisition £(64,000 + 1,200)	(65,200)
Enhancement expenditure (not reflected in value of property on disposal)	(0)
Chargeable gain	**22,300**

Task 2.3

Share pool

	No of Shares	Cost £	Indexed cost £
November 1998	2,000	50,000	50,000
Index to February 2003			
£50,000 × 0.118			5,900
	2,000	50,000	55,900
Rights Issue	1,000	20,000	20,000
	3,000	70,000	75,900
Index to June 2011			
£75,900 × 0.289			21,935
	3,000	70,000	97,835
Less: sale	(2,500)	(58,333)	(81,529)
Carry forward	500	11,667	16,306

Gain		£
Disposal proceeds		102,100
Less: cost		(58,333)
		43,767
Indexation (81,529 – 58,333)		(23,196)
Chargeable gain		20,571

Task 2.4

A and B

Note that gift relief cannot be restricted to allow Sami to use his annual exempt amount.

Task 2.5

(1)

	£
Proceeds of sale	230,000
Less: cost	(120,000)
	110,000
Less: indexation allowance £120,000 × 0.177	(21,240)
Chargeable gain	**88,760**

(2) The dates during which a new asset must be acquired for a rollover relief claim to be made are between **1 May 2010** and **1 May 2014**.

(3)

Gain immediately chargeable £(230,000 – 200,000)	30,000
Gain which can be rolled-over £(88,760 – 30,000)	**58,760**

....

Task 2.6

False

The rights issue shares will be treated as acquired on 10 June 2005 and so will be part of the FA 1985 pool. However, indexation allowance will be applied on the rights issue cost from November 2011.

....

Task 2.7

(1) **£0.00**

Jayden's accounting profit for 2011/12 is less than £5,315 so the small earnings exception applies.

(2) £(7,500 – 7,225) = £275 x 9%   **£24.75**

....

Task 2.8

(1) He should have notified HMRC by 31 January following the tax year in which he started to trade that he was liable to Class 2 contributions, ie by **31 January 2013**.

(2) He should have notified HMRC that he was liable to income tax by **5 October 2012**.

(3) He should have filed his first tax return by **31 January 2013**.

....

Task 2.9

	£
Taxable total profits	139,790
Dividends (£40,500 × 100/90)	45,000
Augmented profits	184,790
£139,790 × 26%	36,345.40
Less: 3/200 (750,000 – 184,790) × $\frac{139,790}{184,790}$	(6,413.55)
Corporation tax payable	29,931.85

Note: Sweet Ltd has one associated company, so

lower limit is £$\frac{300,000}{2}$ = £150,000 and the

upper limit is £$\frac{1,500,000}{2}$ = £750,000

The dividend from the associated company is ignored.

Task 2.10

	True	False
A company with a period of account ending on 30 September 2011 must keep its records until 30 September 2017	✓	
The penalty for failing to keep records is £3,000 for each accounting period	✓	
A sole trader who is seven months late filing a tax return will be subject to a penalty of £200		✓ (£100 plus daily penalty and 5% of tax due)

Task 2.11

Partnership tax adjusted trading profit £(210,000 – 70,000 – 69,710 – 13,200) = £57,090

Page 6

Box 1	01.04.11
Box 2	31.03.12
Box 3	Fishmongers
Box 11	57090.00
Box 6	Fred Fisher
Box 11	38060.00

PRACTICE ASSESSMENT 4
BUSINESS TAX

Time allowed: 2 hours

Taxation tables

Capital allowances

Writing down allowance

Plant and machinery	20%
Annual investment allowance	£100,000

First year allowance

Energy saving and water efficient plant	100%

Motor cars

CO_2 emissions up to 110g/km (low emission cars)	100%
CO_2 emissions between 111g/km and 160g/km	20%
CO_2 emissions over 160g/km	10%

National insurance contributions

Class 2 contributions	£2.50 per week
Small earnings exception	£5,315 per year
Class 4 contributions	
Main rate	9%
Additional rate	2%
Lower profits limit	£7,225
Upper profits limit	£42,475

Corporation tax

Financial year	2011	2010
Small profits rate	20%	21%
Lower limit	300,000	300,000
Upper limit	1,500,000	1,500,000
Standard fraction	3/200	7/400
Main rate	26%	28%

Formula: Fraction × (U − A) × N/A

Capital gains tax

Rate of tax

Standard rate	18%
Higher rate (applicable over £35,000)	28%
Entrepreneurs' relief rate	10%
Annual exempt amount	£10,600
Entrepreneurs' relief	
Lifetime limit	£10,000,000

Business Tax Practice Assessment 4

Section 1

Task 1.1

For the following items of expenditure, tick if they are allowable or disallowable when calculating taxable trading profits:

	Allowable	Disallowable
Replacing roof of premises which was unsound when recently acquired	☐	☑
Fine for breach of health and safety regulations	☐	☑
Legal fees on renewal of ten-year lease	☑	☐

Task 1.2

You work in the tax department of a manufacturing company trading as Hoppings Ltd. The following information is available for the year ended 31 July 2011.

(1) A summary of the accounts show:

	£	£
Gross profit		690,450
Depreciation	45,060	
Expenses	272,100	
Directors' salaries	145,030	
Other salaries	190,990	
		(653,180)
Net profit		37,270

The expenses include:

Legal fees in relation to building purchase	5,400
Speeding fines incurred by a director	200
Gift Aid payment made	1,500

(2) The capital allowances have already been calculated at £52,710.

Using the pro forma layout provided, calculate the adjusted trading profits for the year ended 31 July 2011.

	£	£

Task 1.3

Dilys had been trading for many years until she ceased trading on 30 September 2011. Her recent profits were:

	£
Year ended 31 December 2009	38,400
Year ended 31 December 2010	27,000
Period ended 30 September 2011	12,000 +

Dilys had overlap profits arising from the start of her trade of £6,500.

(1) The tax year of cessation is: [2011/12]

(2) Her taxable profits in the tax year of cessation were:

  A £5,500

  B £6,500

  C £32,500

  D £39,000

(3) Her taxable profits in the tax year before tax year of cessation were:

  A £22,286

  B £27,000

  C £32,700

  D £38,400

(4) Her taxable profits in the tax year which was two years before tax year of cessation were:

A   £26,537

B   £32,700

C   £38,400

D   £31,900

Task 1.4

Osian makes a trading loss of £5,000 in 2011/12. He has property income of £6,300 in 2011/12. Osian had taxable trading income of £10,000 in 2010/11 and property income of £2,000.

True or False: Osian can claim to use his loss of 2011/12 against his general income in 2010/11 only, in order to preserve his personal allowance in 2011/12.

Task 1.5

Adam and Briony have been in partnership for many years making up accounts to 31 December each year. Adam was entitled to a salary of £15,000 a year and they shared the remaining profits equally.

On 1 May 2011, Coral joined the partnership. It was agreed Adam would no longer be entitled to a salary and that profits would be shared 2:2:1 between Adam, Briony and Coral.

For the year ended 31 December 2011, the partnership trading profit was £60,000.

Using the pro forma layout provided, show the division of profit between the partners for the year ended 31 December 2011.

	Total	Adam	Briony	Coral
	£	£	£	£
Period to: 30 April 2011				
SALARY	5000	5000	—	—
PROFIT SHARE 1:1	15000	7500	7500	—
Period to: 31 December 2011				
PROFIT SHARE 2:2:1	40000	16000	16000	8000
Total profit for y/e 31.12.11	60,000	28500	23500	8000

Task 1.6

K Ltd decides to make up accounts for a fifteen month period of account to 30 November 2012. It made a capital gain of £10,000 in January 2012 and a capital gain of £20,000 in October 2012.

True or false: the gain of £10,000 will be dealt with in the accounting period to 31 August 2012 and the gain of £20,000 will be dealt with in the accounting period to 30 November 2012.

Task 1.7

Codie is in business as a sole trader making up accounts to 30 September each year. You have been asked to complete her capital allowances computation for the year to 30 September 2011. The following information is relevant:

(1) The capital allowance computation showed the following written-down value at 30 September 2010:

	£
Main pool	58,060

(2) During the period 1 October 2010 to 30 September 2011, Codie had the following capital transactions:

Purchases		£
November 2010	Plant and machinery	55,030
May 2011	Plant and machinery	8,000
May 2011	Car (CO_2 emissions 140g/km)	19,320 (80% private use)
Disposals		
January 2011	Plant and machinery	23,900

Using the pro forma layout provided, compute Codie's capital allowances computation for the year to 30 September 2011.

Section 2

Task 2.1

For the following items of expenditure, tick if they are allowable when computing a capital gain:

	Allowable	Not allowable
Advertising for buyers	✓	☐
Repainting window frames	☐	✓
Stamp duty payable on acquisition	✓	☐

Task 2.2

FGH plc bought a painting in October 2005 for £3,600. FGH plc sold the painting at auction in September 2011 and received £7,200 after deducting the auctioneers' commission of £800. The indexation factor between October 2005 and September 2011 is 0.204.

Complete the following computation.

	£
Proceeds	
Disposal costs	
Cost of acquisition	
Indexation allowance	
Gain	
Gain using chattel marginal relief	
Actual gain chargeable	

Task 2.3

Ros bought 2,000 shares in Blueberry Ltd for £10,000 in November 2003.

In March 2005, she received 400 shares in a bonus issue. In May 2007 the company offered a rights issue at 1 share for every 6 held. She accepted this rights issue at £3 per share. She sold 1,800 shares in Blueberry Ltd in July 2011 for £13,500.

Using the pro forma layouts provided, show the chargeable gain on sale.

Share pool

	No of shares	Cost £

Gain

	£
Proceeds of sale	
Less: allowable cost	
Chargeable gain	

Task 2.4

In order to claim rollover relief for the reinvestment of a business asset, the reinvestment must take place during what period?

A   The period beginning three years before and ending three years after the date of the disposal

B   The period beginning one year before and ending three years after the date of the disposal

C   The period beginning one year before and ending one year after the date of the disposal

D   The period beginning with the date of disposal and ending three years after the date of the disposal

Task 2.5

Patricia owned 25% of the shares in a company, which qualify for entrepreneurs' relief. Patricia has already made gains of £10,600 on disposals of other investments in July 2011. She is a higher rate taxpayer.

- In June 1987, she bought the shares for £5,000.
- In January 2012, she sold the shares. The gross proceeds were £17,500.
- The selling agent charged her a commission of 5%.

Using the pro forma layout provided, calculate Patricia's capital gains tax liability for 2011/12.

	£

Task 2.6

True or False: if a company makes a trading loss, it cannot set the loss off against its chargeable gains for the same accounting period.

Task 2.7

Abdul is in business as a sole trader. His taxable trading profits for 2011/12 are £56,000, and receives dividends of £9,000 in July 2011.

Abdul's total liability to national insurance contributions for 2011/12 is:

A   £3,773.00

B   £3,443.00

C   £3,573.00

D   £3,643.00

Task 2.8

SR plc makes up accounts to 31 October each year. It pays tax at the small profits rate.

The corporation tax liability of SR plc for the year to 31 October 2011 was £24,000 and for the year to 31 October 2012 was £36,000.

How will SR plc pay the corporation tax liability for the year to 31 October 2012?

A   4 instalments of £6,000 each due on 14 May 2012, 14 August 2012, 14 November 2012 and 14 February 2013, with a balancing payment of £12,000 due on 14 April 2013

B   One payment due on 31 January 2014

C   4 instalments of £9,000 each due on 14 May 2012, 14 August 2012, 14 November 2012 and 14 February 2013

D   One payment due on 1 August 2013

••

Task 2.9

A company has the following information for the year ended 31 March 2012:

(1) Taxable total profits is £535,000
(2) Dividends received, net, are £54,000
(3) The company has one associated company

By filling in the shaded boxes, compute the corporation payable.

£

_____ @   26%   _____

Less:

3/200 × _____   minus _____ ×   _____   _____

Corporation tax payable   _____

••

Task 2.10

Tick the appropriate box for each of the following statements:

	True	False
The maximum penalty for an error in a tax return which is deliberate but not concealed is 75%	☐	☐
If an individual submits his 2011/12 tax return online on 13 January 2013, HMRC can start an enquiry before 31 January 2014	☐	☐
If a company submits its tax return two months late, the penalty is £100	☐	☐

Task 2.11

Complete the following extract from the tax return for Byatt Ltd for the year ended 31 March 2012, using the following information:

	£
Revenue (turnover)	320,000
Trade profits	215,000
Chargeable gain	18,000
Gift Aid donation paid	3,000
Trading loss brought forward	(15,000)
Capital loss brought forward	(2,000)

Page 2

Company tax calculation

Turnover

1	Total turnover from trade or profession	**1** £	

Income

3	Trading and professional profits	**3** £	
4	Trading losses brought forward claimed against profits	**4** £	
5	Net trading and professional profits	box 3 minus box 4 **5** £	
6	Bank, building society or other interest, and profits and gains from non-trading loan relationships	**6** £	
11	Income from UK land and buildings	**11** £	
14	Annual profits and gains not falling under any other heading	**14** £	

Chargeable gains

16	Gross chargeable gains	**16** £	
17	Allowable losses including losses brought forward	**17** £	
18	Net chargeable gains	box 16 minus box 17 **18** £	
21	**Profits before other deductions and reliefs**	sum of boxes 5, 6, 11, 14 & 18 **21** £	

Deductions and Reliefs

24	Management expenses under S75 ICTA 1988	**24** £	
30	Trading losses of this or a later accounting period under S393A ICTA 1988	**30** £	
31	Put an 'X' in box 31 if amounts carried back from later accounting periods are included in box 30	**31**	
32	Non-trade capital allowances	**32** £	
35	Charges paid	**35** £	
37	**Taxable total profits**	box 21 minus boxes 24, 30, 32 and 35 **37** £	

Tax calculation

38	Franked investment income	**38** £	
39	Number of associated companies in this period or	**39**	
40	Associated companies in the first financial year	**40**	
41	Associated companies in the second financial year	**41**	
42	Put an 'X' in box 42 if the company claims to be charged at the starting rate or the small companies' rate on any part of its profits, or is claiming marginal rate relief	**42**	

Enter how much profit has to be charged and at what rate of tax

Financial year (yyyy)	Amount of profit	Rate of tax	Tax	
43	**44** £	**45**	**46** £	p
53	**54** £	**55**	**56** £	p
			total of boxes 46 and 56 **63** £	p

63	Corporation tax		
64	Marginal rate relief	**64** £	p
65	Corporation tax net of marginal rate relief	**65** £	p
66	Underlying rate of corporation tax	**66** • %	
67	Profits matched with non-corporate distributions	**67**	
68	Tax at non-corporate distributions rate	**68** £	p
69	Tax at underlying rate on remaining profits	**69** £	p
70	**Corporation tax chargeable**	See note for box 70 in CT600 Guide **70** £	p

CT600 (Short) (2008) Version 2

PRACTICE ASSESSMENT 4
BUSINESS TAX

ANSWERS

Business Tax Practice Assessment 4 – Answers

Section 1

Task 1.1

For the following items of expenditure, tick if they are allowable or disallowable:

	Allowable	Disallowable
Replacing roof of premises which was unsound when recently acquired		✓
Fine for breach of health and safety regulations		✓
Legal fees on renewal of ten-year lease	✓	

....

Task 1.2

	£	£
Net profit		37,270
Add: depreciation	45,060	
legal fees re building purchase	5,400	
speeding fines	200	
Gift Aid payment	1,500	
		52,160
		89,430
Less: capital allowances		(52,710)
Adjusted trading profit		36,720

....

Task 1.3

(1) **2011/12**

(2) **A**

2011/12

Tax year of cessation: period from start of accounting period to end of accounting period

Basis period 1 January 2011 to 30 September 2011

Taxable trading profits: £12,000 – £6,500 (overlap profits) = £5,500

(3) **B**

2010/11

Tax year before tax year of cessation: current year basis

Basis period 1 January 2010 to 31 December 2010

Taxable trading profits: £27,000

(4) **C**

2009/10

Tax year before tax year of cessation: current year basis

Basis period 1 January 2009 to 31 December 2009

Taxable trading profits: £38,400

Task 1.4

True

Osian can claim to use his loss of 2011/12 against his general income in 2010/11 only, in order to preserve his personal allowance in 2011/12.

Task 1.5

	Total	Adam	Briony	Coral
	£	£	£	£
Period to: 30 April 2011				
Salary (4/12)	5,000	5,000	0	0
Profit share 1:1	15,000	7,500	7,500	0
Period to: 31 December 2011				
Profit share 2:2:1	40,000	16,000	16,000	8,000
Total profit for y/e 31.12.11	60,000	28,500	23,500	8,000

Task 1.6

True

The gain of £10,000 will be dealt with in the accounting period to 31 August 2012 and the gain of £20,000 will be dealt with in the accounting period to 30 November 2012.

Task 1.7

Year ended 30 September 2011

	AIA/FYA	Main pool	Car (20% business)	Allowances
	£	£	£	£
B/f		58,060		
AIA additions				
November 2010	55,030			
May 2011	8,000			
	63,030			
AIA	(63,030)			63,030
	0			
Disposals		(23,900)		
Non-AIA addition				
Car			3,864	
		34,160		
WDA @ 20%		(6,832)	(19,320) × 20%	7,605
		27,328	15,456	70,635

Section 2

Task 2.1

	Allowable	Not allowable
Advertising for buyers	✓	
Repainting window frames		✓ (revenue expense)
Stamp duty payable on acquisition	✓	

Task 2.2

	£
Proceeds	8,000
Disposal costs	(800)
Cost of acquisition	(3,600)
Indexation allowance 0.204 × £3,600	(734)
Gain	2,866
Gain using chattel marginal relief £(8,000 − 6,000) × 5/3	3,333
Actual gain chargeable	2,866

Task 2.3

Share pool

	No of shares	Cost £
11.03 Acquisition	2,000	10,000
3.05 Bonus	400	nil
	2,400	10,000
5.07 Rights 1 for 6 @ £3	400	1,200
	2,800	11,200
7.11 Disposal	(1,800)	(7,200)
c/f	600	4,000

Gain

	£
Proceeds of sale	13,500
Less: allowable cost	(7,200)
Chargeable gain	6,300

....

Task 2.4

B

The period beginning one year before and ending three years after the date of the disposal.

....

Task 2.5

	£
Proceeds	17,500
Less: agent's commission (5%)	(875)
Net proceeds of sale	16,625
Less: cost	(5,000)
Taxable gain (AEA set against other gains of £10,600 realised in July 2011)	11,625
CGT @ 10%	1,162.50

....

Task 2.6

False

A company can set-off its trading loss against total profits in the same accounting period (which includes capital gains).

....

Task 2.7

C

		£
Class 2	NICs (£2.50 × 52)	130.00
Class 4	£(42,475 – 7,225) × 9%	3,172.50
	£(56,000 – 42,475) × 2%	270.50
		3,573.00

....

Task 2.8

D

One payment due on 1 August 2013. Only large companies are required to pay by instalments.

....

Task 2.9

	£
535,000 @ 26%	139,100.00
Less:	
3/200 × 750,000 minus 595,000 × 535,000 / 595,000	(2,090.55)
Corporation tax payable	137,009.45

Notes:

Upper limit £1,500,000/2 = £750,000

Augmented profits are £535,000 + £(54,000 × 100/90) = £595,000

....

Task 2.10

	True	False
The maximum penalty for an error in a tax return which is deliberate but not concealed is 75%		✓ (70%)
If an individual submits his 2011/12 tax return online on 13 January 2013, HMRC can start an enquiry before 31 January 2014		✓ (return submitted by due date: 1 year from actual filing date)
If a company submits its tax return two months late, the penalty is £100	✓	

....

Task 2.11

Box 1	£320000
Box 3 .	£215000
Box 4	£15000
Box 5	£200000
Box 16	£18000
Box 17	£2000
Box 18	£16000
Box 21	£216000
Box 35	£3000
Box 37	£213000
Box 42	X
Box 43	2011
Box 44	£213000
Box 45	20%
Box 46	£42600.00
Box 63	£42600.00
Box 70	£42600.00

••

PRACTICE ASSESSMENT 5
BUSINESS TAX

Time allowed: 2 hours

Taxation tables

Capital allowances

Writing down allowance

Plant and machinery	20%
Annual investment allowance	£100,000

First year allowance

Energy saving and water efficient plant	100%

Motor cars

CO_2 emissions up to 110g/km (low emission cars)	100%
CO_2 emissions between 111g/km and 160g/km	20%
CO_2 emissions over 160g/km	10%

National insurance contributions

Class 2 contributions	£2.50 per week
Small earnings exception	£5,315 per year
Class 4 contributions	
Main rate	9%
Additional rate	2%
Lower profits limit	£7,225
Upper profits limit	£42,475

Corporation tax

Financial year	2011	2010
Small profits rate	20%	21%
Lower limit	300,000	300,000
Upper limit	1,500,000	1,500,000
Standard fraction	3/200	7/400
Main rate	26%	28%

Formula: Fraction × (U − A) × N/A

Capital gains tax

Rate of tax

Standard rate	18%
Higher rate (applicable over £35,000)	28%
Entrepreneurs' relief rate	10%
Annual exempt amount	£10,600
Entrepreneurs' relief	
Lifetime limit	£10,000,000

Business Tax Practice Assessment 5

Section 1

Task 1.1

For the following items of expenditure, tick if they are revenue or capital:

	Revenue	Capital
New machine for factory	☑	☐
Electricity bill for shop lighting	☐	☐
Extension for factory	☐	☐

••

Task 1.2

The income statement (profit and loss account) of Jeremy Ltd for the year to 31 March 2012 shows the following information:

	£	£
Gross profit		512,500
Profit on sale of shares		13,550
Dividends received		6,300
Interest income		4,500
		536,850
General expenses (Note 1)	240,780	
Motor expenses (Note 2)	10,500	
Wages and salaries	110,350	
Administrative expenses	77,230	
Depreciation	15,700	
		(454,560)
Net profit		82,290

Notes

(1) **General expenses**

These include:

	£
Gift Aid donation (paid August 2011)	500
Entertaining customers	9,550
Entertaining staff	8,650

(2) Motor expenses

These include:

	£
Parking fines incurred by director	610
Petrol used by director for private use	6,300
Leasing costs of car for director (CO_2 emissions 180 g/km)	9,300

(3) Capital allowances

The capital allowances for the year ended 31 March 2012 are £8,750

Using the pro forma layout provided, compute the adjusted trading profit for Jeremy Ltd for the year to 31 March 2012.

	£	£

Task 1.3

Logan started trading on 1 March 2011. He made up his first set of accounts to 30 September 2012 and thereafter to 30 September each year. The profits were calculated as

	£
Period to 30 September 2012	38,000
Year to 30 September 2013	36,000

(1) His taxable profits in his first tax year of trading were:

   A   £2,000

   B   £3,000

   C   £14,000

   D   £24,000

(2) His taxable profits in his second tax year of trading were:

   A   £14,000

   B   £24,000

   C   £36,000

   D   £38,000

(3) His taxable profits in his third tax year of trading were:

   A   £24,000

   B   £30,000

   C   £36,000

   D   £38,000

(4) His overlap profits are: £ [   ]

Task 1.4

True or False: when a trading loss is carried back by a company, it is set-off after deducting Gift Aid donations.

Task 1.5

Xavier, Yvonne and Zebedee have been in partnership for many years making up accounts to 30 September each year. Under the partnership agreement, Xavier is entitled to a salary of £9,000 a year and the profits are then divided 2:2:1 between the partners respectively.

Xavier retired from the partnership on 31 December 2011. Yvonne and Zebedee carried on the partnership and the partnership agreement was altered so that the profits were then divided 2:1 between Yvonne and Zebedee respectively.

The partnership profits for the year to 30 September 2012 were £209,000.

(1) Using the pro forma layout provided, show the division of the partnership profit to 30 September 2012.

	Total	Xavier	Yvonne	Zebedee
	£	£	£	£

You see from your files that Xavier's share of the partnership profit for the year to 30 September 2011 was £21,000 and that he had overlap profits of £4,500 on commencement.

(2) Xavier's taxable partnership profits for the tax year of cessation are:

£ [ ]

Task 1.6

When a company has a period of account which exceeds 12 months, how are the following apportioned:

	Time apportioned	Period in which arises/paid	Period in which accrued
Trading income	☐	☐	☐
Gift Aid donation	☐	☐	☐
Property income	☐	☐	☐
Chargeable gain	☐	☐	☐
Interest income	☐	☐	☐

Task 1.7

Mustafa has been trading for many years, making up accounts to 30 April.

His capital allowances balances brought forward at 1 May 2010 were as follows:

Main pool	£3,291
Car for Mustafa, 30% private usage	£8,745

The following capital transactions were made in the period:

Additions		£
10.09.10	Plant and machinery	58,100
15.01.11	Car for Mustafa, CO_2 emissions 100 g/km, 40% private usage	24,500
22.04.11	Plant and machinery	65,000
Disposal		
15.01.11	Mustafa's previous car	8,000
3.02.11	Plant and machinery (original cost £4,100)	5,970

Using the pro forma layout provided, calculate the capital allowances for the year ended 30 April 2011.

	AIA	Main pool	Private use car (70%)	Private use car (60%)	Allowances
	£	£	£	£	£

Section 2

Task 2.1

For each statement, tick the appropriate box relating to the calculation of capital gains.

Disposal	Market value used	Actual proceeds used	No gain/no loss disposal
Ruth gives an asset worth £4,000 to her friend Delwyn	☐	☐	☐
Kai sells land to his sister for £20,000 when it is worth £15,000	☐	☐	☐
John sells shares for £2,000 to his wife Elaine when they are worth £6,000	☐	☐	☐
Gerry sells shares for proceeds of £15,000 to a buyer who he had not previously known	☐	☐	☐

Task 2.2

You have received the following e-mail from Dorothy.

From:	Dorothy@hotbox.net
To:	AATstudent@boxmail.net
Sent:	13 June 2012
Subject:	Help

I know that you are currently dealing with our tax affairs and wondered if you could help us with some advice.

The business is doing really well this year and we want to expand by investing some money. I own a block of four offices and I am happy to sell one of them so that I can put some money into the business but I am worried that I will need to pay a lot of tax on any money that I make.

I bought the offices for £250,000 and the bigger one has a market value of about £150,000. The other three are worth about £350,000 between them.

I would therefore be grateful if you could explain to me what the tax implications of selling the office for £150,000 would be, so that I can make an informed decision on the best thing to do.

Much appreciated

Dorothy

Reply to Dorothy's e-mail, explaining the capital gains tax implications if she sells the office. Assume that rollover relief will not be available on this gain. Dorothy has always been a higher rate taxpayer.

From:	AATstudent@boxmail.net
To:	Dorothy@hotbox.net
Sent:	13 June 2012
Subject:	Re: Help

This page is for the continuation of your e-mail. You may not need all of it.

Task 2.3

In May 2011, Speedy Ltd bought 4,000 shares in Slow Ltd for £9,320. In September 2011 Slow Ltd issued bonus shares of 1 for 40. In January 2012, Speedy Ltd sold 2,350 of these shares for £2.98 each.

Using the pro forma layout provided, show the share pool and compute the gain on the sale in January 2012.

Indexation factor

May 2011 – January 2012   0.026

Share pool

	No of shares	Cost	Indexed cost
		£	£

Gain

	£

Task 2.4

An individual made a capital gain of £2,350,000 in August 2011 on the sale of his business. This was the first disposal that he had made. He has £10,000 of his basic rate band unused in 2011/12

The capital gains tax payable for 2011/12 is:

A   £233,940.00

B   £657,000.00

C   £654,032.00

D   £235,000.00

Task 2.5

Dunray Ltd bought trading premises in July 2003 and sold them on 10 April 2011 for £190,000 realising a gain of £80,000.

Tick the box if a rollover relief claim to defer the whole or part of the gain on disposal can be made in relation to each of the following acquisitions:

Acquisition

Fixed plant and machinery bought in February 2010 for £200,000 ☐

Office building bought in August 2013 for £150,000 ☐

Land bought in December 2011 for £100,000 ☐

Tractors bought in January 2011 for £200,000 ☐

Task 2.6

True or False: indexation allowance is not available on costs of disposal.

Task 2.7

Margie is a sole trader. Her taxable trading profits for the year to 30 September 2011 are £25,560.

Margie's total NICs for 2011/12 are: 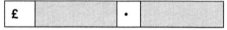 £ [   ] • [   ]

Task 2.8

(1) By what date must a taxpayer generally submit a tax return for 2011/12 if it is filed online?

    A   30 September 2012

    B   31 October 2012

    C   31 December 2012

    D   31 January 2013

(2) On which dates are payment on accounts due for 2011/12?

    A   31 January 2012 and 31 July 2012

    B   31 January 2013 and 31 July 2013

    C   31 July 2012 and 31 January 2013

    D   31 October 2012 and 31 January 2013

Task 2.9

Rothcom Ltd made up accounts for the ten-month period from 1 May 2011 to 28 February 2012. It had taxable total profits of £782,355.

The corporation tax payable by Rothcom Ltd for the period is:

£ [   ] . [   ]

Task 2.10

(1) The maximum penalty for failure to keep records for each tax year or accounting period is:

    A   £4,000

    B   £3,000

    C   £2,500

    D   £1,500

(2) The maximum penalty for a deliberate but not concealed failure to notify chargeability as a percentage of Potential Lost Revenue is:

    A   70%

    B   35%

    C   20%

    D   15%

(3) A taxpayer files his tax return for 2011/12 online on 15 March 2013. His tax liability for the year is £2,000.

The maximum penalty for late filing is:

    A   £2,000

    B   £300

    C   £200

    D   £100

Task 2.11

Paolo has been in business as a tree surgeon for four years and made up his latest set of accounts for the year to 30 September 2011.

The following information is relevant to this period of account:

	£
Revenue (turnover)	90,000
Wages – Paolo	20,000
Wages – other staff	42,000
Travel (10% private)	10,700
Insurance	9,800
Office costs	1,800
Bank charges	200
Accountancy	650
Machinery purchased	15,000

Using this information, complete the self-employment page that follows.

Business expenses

Read pages SEFN 7 to SEFN 9 of the *notes* to see what expenses are allowable for tax purposes.

Total expenses	Disallowable expenses
If your annual turnover was below £73,000 you may just put your total expenses in box 30	Use this column if the figures in boxes 16 to 29 include disallowable amounts

16 Cost of goods bought for resale or goods used

£ [   ] · 0 0

31

£ [   ] · 0 0

17 Construction industry - *payments to subcontractors*

£ [   ] · 0 0

32

£ [   ] · 0 0

18 Wages, salaries and other staff costs

£ [   ] · 0 0

33

£ [   ] · 0 0

19 Car, van and travel expenses

£ [   ] · 0 0

34

£ [   ] · 0 0

20 Rent, rates, power and insurance costs

£ [   ] · 0 0

35

£ [   ] · 0 0

21 Repairs and renewals of property and equipment

£ [   ] · 0 0

36

£ [   ] · 0 0

22 Phone, fax, stationery and other office costs

£ [   ] · 0 0

37

£ [   ] · 0 0

23 Advertising and business entertainment costs

£ [   ] · 0 0

38

£ [   ] · 0 0

24 Interest on bank and other loans

£ [   ] · 0 0

39

£ [   ] · 0 0

25 Bank, credit card and other financial charges

£ [   ] · 0 0

40

£ [   ] · 0 0

26 Irrecoverable debts written off

£ [   ] · 0 0

41

£ [   ] · 0 0

27 Accountancy, legal and other professional fees

£ [   ] · 0 0

42

£ [   ] · 0 0

28 Depreciation and loss/profit on sale of assets

£ [   ] · 0 0

43

£ [   ] · 0 0

29 Other business expenses

£ [   ] · 0 0

44

£ [   ] · 0 0

30 Total expenses in boxes 16 to 29

£ [   ] · 0 0

45 Total disallowable expenses in boxes 31 to 44

£ [   ] · 0 0

PRACTICE ASSESSMENT 5
BUSINESS TAX

ANSWERS

Business Tax Practice Assessment 5 – Answers

Section 1

Task 1.1

	Revenue	Capital
New machine for factory		✓
Electricity bill for shop lighting	✓	
Extension for factory		✓

∙∙∙

Task 1.2

Jeremy Ltd adjusted trading profit for the year ending 31 March 2012

		£	£
Net profit			82,290
Add:	Gift Aid donation	500	
	entertaining customers	9,550	
	fines for director	610	
	leasing costs £9,300 × 15%	1,395	
	depreciation	15,700	
			27,755
			110,045
Less:	profit on sale of shares	13,550	
	dividends received	6,300	
	interest income	4,500	
	capital allowances	8,750	
			(33,100)
Adjusted trading profit			76,945

∙∙∙

Task 1.3

(1) **A**

2010/11

First tax year: actual basis

Basis period: 1 March 2011 to 5 April 2011

Taxable trading profits: $1/19 \times £38,000 = £2,000$

(2) **B**

2011/12

Second tax year: actual basis

Basis period: 6 April 2011 to 5 April 2012

Taxable trading profits: $12/19 \times £38,000 = £24,000$

(3) **A**

2012/13

Third tax year: period of 12 months to accounting date ending in tax year

Basis period: 1 October 2011 to 30 September 2012

Taxable trading profits: $12/19 \times £38,000 = £24,000$

(4) Overlap period: 1 October 2011 to 5 April 2012

Overlap profits: $6/19 \times £38,000 = $ **£12,000**

. . . .

Task 1.4

False

When a trading loss is carried back by a company, it is set-off **before** deducting Gift Aid donations.

. . . .

Task 1.5

(1)

	Total	Xavier	Yvonne	Zebedee
	£	£	£	£
Period to 31.12.11				
Salary × 3/12	2,250	2,250	0	0
Profits 2:2:1	50,000	20,000	20,000	10,000
Period to 30.9.12				
Profits 2:1	156,750	0	104,500	52,250
Total profit for y/e 30.9.12	209,000	22,250	124,500	62,250

(2)

2011/12	£
Profit for y/e 30 September 2011	21,000
Profit for p/e 31 December 2011	22,250
Less: overlap profit	(4,500)
Taxable profit for 2011/12	**38,750**

....

Task 1.6

	Time apportioned	Period in which arises/paid	Period in which accrued
Trading income	✓		
Gift Aid donation		✓	
Property income	✓		
Chargeable gain		✓	
Interest income			✓

....

Task 1.7

Year ended 30 April 2011

	AIA	Main pool	Private use car (70%)	Private use car (60%)	Allowances
	£	£	£	£	£
b/f		3,291	8,745		
AIA additions					
September 2010	58,100				
April 2011	65,000				
	123,100				
AIA	(100,000)				100,000
	23,100				
Transfer to pool	(23,100)				
		23,100			
Non-AIA				24,500	
Car January 11					
Disposals		(4,100)	(8,000)		
		22,291			
BA			745 × 70%		522
WDA @ 20%		(4,458)			4,458
FYA @ 100%				(24,500) × 60%	14,700
c/f		17,833		0	
Total allowances					119,680

....

Section 2

Task 2.1

Disposal	Market value used	Actual proceeds used	No gain/no loss disposal
Ruth gives an asset worth £4,000 to her friend Delwyn	✓		
Kai sells land to his sister for £20,000 when it is worth £15,000	✓		
John sells shares for £2,000 to his wife Elaine when they are worth £6,000			✓
Gerry sells shares for proceeds of £15,000 to a buyer who he had not previously known		✓	

•••

Task 2.2

First, a tax computation would be done, which allows you to deduct the cost of the office.

Based on your figures, this would be:

	£
Proceeds	150,000
Less: cost £250,000 × $\dfrac{150,000}{150,000 + 350,000}$	(75,000)
Gain	75,000

From this figure, you can then deduct the annual exempt amount of £10,600 and then the remaining figure is taxable at the rate of 28%. The tax due would be £18,032.

Therefore, given that you will receive £150,000 from the sale of the office, the after tax proceeds should exceed £130,000.

•••

Task 2.3

Share pool

	No of shares	Cost	Indexed cost
		£	£
May 2011	4,000	9,320	9,320
September 2011 Bonus issue	100	–	–
	4,100	9,320	9,320
Indexation allowance £9,320 × 0.026			242
			9,562
Disposal	(2,350)	(5,342)	(5,481)
Pool to carry forward	1,750	3,978	4,081

Gain

	£
Proceeds £2.98 × 2,350	7,003
Less: cost	(5,342)
	1,661
Less: indexation allowance £(5,481 – 5,342)	(139)
	1,522

. . . .

Task 2.4

A

£(2,350,000 – 10,600) x 10% = £233,940

Lifetime limit for entrepreneurs' relief is £10,000,000

. . . .

Task 2.5

Acquisition	
Fixed plant and machinery bought in February 2010 for £200,000	More than one year before disposal
Office building bought in August 2013 for £150,000	✓ partial relief available
Land bought in December 2011 for £100,000	Amount not reinvested is more than gain
Tractors bought in January 2011 for £200,000	Moveable plant is not a qualifying asset

Task 2.6

True

Indexation allowance is not available on costs of disposal.

Task 2.7

	£
Class 2: £2.50 × 52	130.00
Class 4: £(25,560 – 7,225) = £18,335 × 9%	1,650.15
	1,780.15

Task 2.8

(1) **D**

Online returns for 2011/12 must usually be submitted by 31 January 2013.

(2) **A**

Payments on account are due on 31 January in the tax year and 31 July following the end of the tax year.

Task 2.9

	£
£782,355 × 26%	203,412.30
Less: marginal relief ((1,500,000 × 10/12) – 782,355) × 3/200	(7,014.68)
Corporation tax payable	196,397.62

Task 2.10

(1) **B**

The maximum penalty for failure to keep records for each tax year or accounting period is £3,000.

(2) **A**

The maximum penalty for a deliberate but not concealed failure as a percentage of Potential Lost Revenue is 70%.

(3) **D**

Initial penalty for filing return late is £100. As it is less than 3 months late no further penalty is payable.

Task 2.11

Box 18	£62000.00
Box 19	£10700.00
Box 20	£9800.00
Box 22	£1800.00
Box 25	£200.00
Box 27	£650.00
Box 30	£85150.00
Box 33	£20000.00
Box 34	£1070.00
Box 45	£21070.00

Taxation tables

Capital allowances

Writing down allowance

Plant and machinery	20%
Annual investment allowance	£100,000

First year allowance

Energy saving and water efficient plant	100%

Motor cars

CO_2 emissions up to 110g/km (low emission cars)	100%
CO_2 emissions between 111g/km and 160g/km	20%
CO_2 emissions over 160g/km	10%

National insurance contributions

Class 2 contributions	£2.50 per week
Small earnings exception	£5,315 per year
Class 4 contributions	
Main rate	9%
Additional rate	2%
Lower profits limit	£7,225
Upper profits limit	£42,475

Corporation tax

Financial year	2011	2010
Small profits rate	20%	21%
Lower limit	300,000	300,000
Upper limit	1,500,000	1,500,000
Standard fraction	3/200	7/400
Main rate	26%	28%

Taxation tables

Formula: Fraction × (U − A) × N/A

Capital gains tax

Rate of tax

Standard rate	18%
Higher rate (applicable over £35,000)	28%
Entrepreneurs' relief rate	10%

Annual exempt amount	£10,600

Entrepreneurs' relief

Lifetime limit	£10,000,000

Notes

Notes

Notes

Notes

Notes

Notes